THE

CEREAL TYCOON

THE
CEREAL TYCOON

~•~

HENRY PARSONS CROWELL
Founder of the Quaker Oats Co.
—— A BIOGRAPHY ——

JOE MUSSER

MOODY PRESS
CHICAGO

ISBN: 0-8024-1616-0

1 3 5 7 9 10 8 6 4 2

Printed in the United States of America

An Introduction
to the Crowell Trust

Only in a few instances is it true that individuals make significant contributions to society after more than forty years in their professional field. For most in their seventies momentum begins to slow, enthusiasm fade, and dreams are tossed one by one into the ashbin. But not so in 1927 for Henry Parsons Crowell, born January 27th, 1855. He had already been successful in developing the Wyoming Hereford Breeding Ranch, a Percheron horse breeding farm, the Perfection Stove Company, and known internationally as founder of the Quaker Oats Company.

While Chairman of the Moody Bible Institute's Board of Directors, still active on corporate boards and the Chicago Board of Trade, the Lord whom he dearly loved and had so faithfully served, gave Henry a new vision. It was the concept of establishing a trust with some of the funds with which he had been blessed, a vehicle which could if properly developed and managed, serve God's work in perpetuity. This became another step in his lifetime of signal dedication and commitment to the Lord. It was always Henry's wishes that his name be kept in the background and that Christ always be preeminent in connection with monies granted. His son, Coleman Crowell, became the first Chairman of the Board, serving for 38 years.

For any who have studied the Crowell Trust Indenture, it represents spiritual wisdom and much prayer, a document that conveys a message as relevant and clear as when it was written in 1927. It reflects the wishes of a biblically conservative man who was compelled to invest and manage funds for the purpose of "encouraging and promoting the spread of Evangelical Chrisitanity." The Crowell Trust is the story of a man's faith-walk that led to a far-reaching decision, made with uncanny insight because of dependence for wisdom promised from the Lord he trusted and served.

The guidelines set forth in the Indenture for original and future Trustees have been faithfully followed, believing that he had divine guidance in writing it. It has not become dated but remains a very clear directive in complete harmony with God's word. The current board of five trustees state, "It is explicit to the point of ease in following and carrying out Mr. Crowell's wishes to honor the Lord whom he loved and served during his life on this earth."

For more than 75 years Trustees have made grants to hundreds of Christian ministries serving Jesus Christ around the world. The income from the Trust, and occasionally funds from the principal, are prayerfully expended to evangelical organizations whose mission is compatible with that of the Indenture. These include upper-level academic institutions, home and foreign missions, and service organizations performing a very wide variety of ministry. Currently, an average of 125 to 150 grants totaling $4 to $5.5 million are made annually.

As of this writing, there have been a total of 19 Trustees, including Mr. Crowell, averaging almost 17 years of service each.

JTB

Foreword

To my right in the lobby where I await the elevator to my office each morning hangs a plaque. The next time you visit the Moody campus, I invite you to pause for a moment to read the short inscription*. You will appreciate it more after reading the book you hold in your hands right now.

The legacy of Henry Parson Crowell continues to this very hour, more than 50 years since his passing into glory. Through the business activity of the Quaker Oats Company, the various ministries of Moody Bible Institute, and the generosity of Henry Parson Crowell for the many works that he started through the Crowell Trust at the turn of the century all continue, having been built on a solid foundation.

Author Joe Musser has done a remarkable job of capturing the heart and soul of Crowell in this new biography. Men and women alike will be inspired and challenged by Crowell's work ethic and commitment to Jesus Christ. Like all good biographies, readers will gain a sense of history and of a different era when life seemed harder in many ways.

Half a century ago, Richard Ellsworth Day's classic work on Crowell's life, *Breakfast Table Autocrat,* inspired readers of that generation to see their life and career as means for the advancement of the cause of Christ. I trust this fresh writing will have the same impact on you.

Joseph M. Stowell
The President
Moody Bible Institute

* *"If my life can always be lived so as to please Him in every way, I'll be supremely happy."*--Henry Parsons Crowell

3

Introduction

As a leading statesman of both big business and evangelical Christianity, Henry Parsons Crowell was a famous figure in both worlds. He founded the Quaker Oats Company and made a fortune in several other businesses.

His philanthropy is well known. Having read an earlier biography of Henry Parsons Crowell 35 years ago, I felt that this man and his life had something significant then to say to "movers and shakers" of my generation. It still has something to say to contemporary readers.

It may be somewhat presumptuous to write a detailed biography of a man who died over 50 years ago. He is no longer available for interviews--even his contemporaries are gone, for the most part.

Fortunately, material exists which documents most of the events and activities of his life. It wasn't difficult capturing these and laying them out chronologically. But what was more complicated was trying to capture the personality, thoughts and spirit of the man.

These qualities, as well as Mr. Crowell's essential character, are quite clear. He had, after all, a dramatic impact on the lives of thousands of people. In fact, it would not be out of line to even say *millions* of people. As the founder of Quaker Oats Company, he was the man who helped change the breakfast habits of almost all Americans, and in the process helped to create entirely new methods of marketing and merchandising that are still revolutionary, even by today's standards.

Henry Parsons Crowell became enormously wealthy because of his business successes. But it is *what he did with his wealth*, and the stewardship of his time and money that holds such interest and value for today's readers.

Here is the setting. It was just before a new century. There were dramatic technological changes making old jobs obsolete; business and industry were in turmoil. Through increasing mergers and acquisitions, tens of thousands of workers lost their jobs when businesses consolidated by using the new technology. Sound familiar?

Steam engines, telegraph and telephone systems, electricity--even something as simple as a typewriter--were changes as revolutionary at the end of the 19th century as communications satellites, jet planes, computers, credit cards and cyber space are at the end of this 20th Century.

Henry Crowell's remarkable life spanned that period. Born just before the Civil War, he lived almost 90 years, to the last days of World War II. This era was a time of unbelievable, exciting and frightening events. As Mr. Crowell approached the new century, he was not afraid of this explosion in industrial technology. In fact, he harnessed the changes, took advantage of the resulting new opportunities, then helped to confront the fears that these changes created.

Henry Crowell learned how to listen, persevere, then address the challenges and mediate the conflicts between those who wanted to keep the traditions of the old century and those who pushed for the ways of the future. In so doing, he has become a role model for our own age.

In writing this biography, we used the literary form of the historical/biographical novel as our model to capture the drama and emotions of Mr. Crowell's life. Even though much material exists which records the actual events, words and activities of Henry Parsons Crowell, it is not possible to find every conversation documented. Yet research gave us an understanding of the man and his experiences in order to re-create these scenes and events. While the historical or biographical novel often uses fiction to embellish the story, this is not the case with this biography. Rather, it is simply the style of writing used, and no liberties were consciously taken with the truth or actual events in his life; these really needed no embellishment.

Some readers may be unfamiliar with the ethos and language of his earliest days, yet it is the structure upon which this exciting true life adventure is built. The early chapters of this biography create this foundation that is necessary to understand the man and his life.

We appreciate the work of earlier biographers, Richard Ellsworth Day, (*Breakfast Table Autocrat*, 1946, Moody Press); Faith Cox Bailey, (*The Man Who Knew the Meaning of Hard Work*, WMBI Radio Drama Series, "Stories of Great Christians") and Arthur F. Marquette, (*Brands, Tradmarks and Good Will: The Story of The Quaker Oats Company*, McGraw Hill Book Company) in providing other dimensions to the life of Mr. Crowell. We also wish to express our thanks to Perry Straw of Moody Bible Institute for his assistance and to the Crowell Trust, which allowed us access to other important research.

-- Joe Musser
January, 1997

"Teach us to number our days and recognize how few they are; help us to spend them as we should. Satisfy us in our earliest youth with your lovingkindness, giving us constant joy to the end of our lives."
(Psalm 90:12,14, Living Bible)

"You alone are my God; my times are in your hands." *(Psalm 31:15, Living Bible)*

Chapter One

America was hardly a generation old when Henry Luther Crowell took his wife, Anna Eliza (Parsons) and left New England for the primitive territory of the Western Reserve. As part of its gains of the Revolution, America had acquired over a quarter million square miles of this land in 1783 from Britain as part of the Treaty of Paris settlement of the war. Luther* wasn't born until 1824, but the idea of claiming frontier land and starting a business was fresh and exciting--as it had been at the beginning of the new nation.

Tens of thousands of pioneers had already spread out across the Allegheny Mountains and onto the rich farmlands of Pennsylvania and Ohio. Some ventured to the far outposts of the Territory, to Indiana, Kentucky and Illinois. Still others took to the seas, all the way around the tip of South America up to the gold fields of California where the famous strike at Sutter's Mill had been made just four years earlier.

Luther, 29, and his bride, four years younger, had set out from Hartford, Connecticut in the spring of 1853. The couple was among the first to use the brand new four-horse stagecoach which covered the distance more speedily than "old fashioned" ox drawn covered wagons or the one or two horse carriages.

Inside the coach, Anna looked out the window at the blooming lilacs and leafing oaks as the stagecoach rolled over the rutted road. The sun was bright and she was encouraged. The young woman was still a radiant bride.

Slight but shapely, Anna had an aristocratic beauty that had first captured Luther's eyes, then his heart. She wore a bonnet, but it did not completely hide her dark brown curls. Her matching brown eyes, wide and innocent, often

*Henry Luther Crowell was probably called by his given name, but to avoid confusion in this biography, he shall be called Luther.

7

had people mistaking her for a girl and not the wife of the man on the seat across from her. Luther was napping but stirred slightly when the coach bumped and slid over a muddy rise in the road.

Anna reflected over the whirlwind activities of the past year. She'd met Luther in Connecticut where he courted her then asked her father for her hand. All during their courtship Luther Crowell, a slender young Yankee with dark flashing eyes and thick black hair and sideburns after the fashion of the day, entranced her with stories of the new lands to the west.

Luther always dressed in a manner that gave him the appearance and sophistication of a leader. He seldom appeared in public without coat and tie. But lest his public presence give him an aura of arrogance or make him seem pompous, Luther's hair had an unruly quality that gave balance, softening his presence. His ears stuck out just enough to keep him from seeming too handsome. His often wild, gesturing hands animated his conversations, and yet everyone felt comfortable in Luther's presence.

Luther had told Anna about the towns and cities of the Western Reserve and further beyond that, in the Northwest Territory. He had gotten his hands on as many reports and books as he could, and many evenings they discussed places that seemed so exotic. Finally, he had narrowed down his choices.

"I think it'll either be Madison city in the Wisconsin Territory. Or, maybe Cleveland, on the banks of the Erie Lake," he had told her. "One of these will be our new home. We'll settle in Cleveland first, 'cause it's closer. Maybe we'll stay there. If we don't like it, then we'll go west some more."

Anna smiled. As the stagecoach rolled along, she enjoyed her memories, recalling his serious determination and excitement. Frankly, she hadn't really cared where in the world Luther went, as long as he took her with him. They were married in a small but elegant ceremony in Hartford, just before the autumn chills of October. They spent the cold, winter months preparing for their journey.

Now, looking out the window, Anna saw that there were more signs of activity. Carriages, men on horseback, people walking alongside the road. Luther stirred from his nap, then looked outside. "We must be there!" he exclaimed. They had arrived in Cleveland on schedule--May 16, 1853.

Luther and Anna had each come from well-to-do families and it's likely they could have remained in New England with many others of the early aristocracy, but Luther strongly felt something calling them westward.

General Moses Cleaveland* had founded this small settlement, which he'd named for himself, on the banks of Lake Erie. Now, fifty years later, it was a thriving community. There was a boomtown quality of growth and the population had doubled in the last five years--now with over 25,000 souls.

The young bride and groom quickly found a house for sale on Sheriff Street, right on the town square and near the Presbyterian Church. Not long afterward, Luther went into business. He formed a partnership with another young pioneer, John Seymour and the two men started a wholesale shoe business and began selling to the burgeoning population. Almost immediately they prospered.

Seymour & Crowell started in business the summer of 1854, at a most pivotal time in the shoe manufacturing industry. Four years later, the invention of a Massachusetts shoemaker would revolutionize the business by eliminating the time-consuming hard work of hand sewing shoe leather.

Machines helped them make shoes better and faster than before, and the business grew beyond their greatest dreams. (In fact, the business would last for over a century, although through a succession of names: *Seymour & Crowell, Crowell & Childs,* finally, *A. O. Childs.*)

An enterprising newspaper editor found that Cleaveland's name had one too many letters for the masthead and he shortened it to the present spelling by dropping the "a".

9

The Cereal Tycoon

By 1856, the settlement of Cleveland was 50 years old but incorporated as a town just 20 years earlier. Still, the population was already over 33,000 and exploding daily. Cleveland had grown by 8,000 since their arrival a year earlier.

(The same year that Luther and Anna moved here, another family also came. William and Eliza Rockefeller moved to Cleveland from New York, along with their son, John Davison. They were part of the business and society life of the city, but it would be the son--John D. Rockefeller--who would leave his mark, not just on the Crowell family and Cleveland, but the whole world, as unfolds in this story some years later.)

Luther and Anna, both of whom could trace their ancestry back hundreds of years, were also well known in society life. Yet, it wasn't something they sought out. Luther was more interested in making the church the central part of their life. He made sure that faith was a part of their growing family. Their new pastor, Dr. James Eells, was about Luther's age, so the two men formed a friendship that gave great meaning to each of them in years to come.

As Luther's business grew, he became more and more prosperous. For their house, they acquired furniture from the East and real carpets for the floors. Anna busied herself in decorating the house and making it a home. She became involved with the church. Before long, both Luther and Anna had given up any thoughts of moving further west to Madison.

Anna worried about one aspect of their move to Ohio, however. The icy cold winters of Cleveland were even more bone-chilling than those of New England. The winds roared continuously across Lake Erie, dumping amazing amounts of snow on the small city. Often it took days to clear paths to the general store or church.

In Hartford, Luther had suffered from "lung trouble". His regular bouts with the disease left him so weak that he had to give up plans to attend Yale. In fact, any kind of college education was out of the question, so he had resigned himself to making his mark in the business world.

Now, Anna thought of her husband's frail health as she carried a bowl of hot soup to his bedroom where he lay recuperating from a current winter bout of "lung trouble". Luther weakly sat up as Anna propped and fluffed his pillows but even that little effort triggered another coughing fit.

Anna gave him a drink of water and it helped. He took the soup bowl and began to feed himself. "Reckon I'm some better," he said a few minutes later.

Anna nodded, wiping his brow with a cool wash cloth. "Soon it'll be spring and you'll be better--just like last year," she offered. "Seems like the sickness just hangs on all winter and then you get better."

Luther finished the soup, put the bowl on the tray and lay back on the pillow. He closed his eyes and breathed hoarsely but didn't cough for a long time.

Anna's prediction was correct. By spring, Luther was able to spend more time at work and less in bed recovering. The sunny, warm days encouraged him. Despite his health problems, the business flourished.

It was ironic, though--now that it was summer and Luther was feeling better, Anna was strangely ill. A year after arriving in Cleveland, she found herself throwing up and feeling quite queasy for no apparent reason. Then she learned the reason--she was going to have a baby.

As Anna's abdomen grew bigger with the passing months, she somehow put aside her own needs to once again tend to her husband. As winter once again dumped snow and cold upon Cleveland, Luther's lung trouble afflicted him. Somehow, though, he rallied when January 27 came and it was time for his pretty young wife to deliver.

Dr. Naught*, the family doctor, parked his horse and carriage outside the small home on Sheriff Street and he went in

*The actual name of the family physician is lost in history.

to check on Anna. She had already begun her labor and had been having real contractions for several hours. A neighbor woman, standing by to act as midwife if the doctor hadn't come, helped Anna during the contractions.

Luther put more wood in the fireplace and the cookstove in the kitchen, warming the house for the birthing. Then, he paced outside the bedroom, praying for his wife. There were always complications that could overwhelm young mothers in situations like this, of course. True, fewer women were dying in childbirth these days than in the previous century, but there were still enough as to energize his prayers. Luther looked up from his vigil after awhile and watched the few people outside on the street in their comings and goings as the hours passed ever so slowly. Finally, he heard a slight commotion in the bedroom, followed by a fairly loud squalling.

Dr. Naught came out after another half hour, drying his hands on a small linen towel. "Anna's fine, Luther. Just fine. So is the baby."

"Thank God," Luther sighed.

"And you've got a nice strong boy. You can hear him yellin'," the doctor smiled. "D'ya know what you're gonna call him yet?"

Luther grinned and nodded. "We said if it was a boy, we'd call him Henry Parsons--after his mother's family."

"Nice name." Dr. Naught came over to where Luther was sitting. "And how are *you* doin'? Still havin' trouble with your lungs?"

"Not so bad," Luther answered with little conviction. "I haven't thought much about it lately, in all the excitement. I've just learned to kind of take it easy during the bad weather."

The doctor didn't say anything, but bent slightly to examine Luther's eyes, ears and throat. "When you go out, be sure to wear a muffler over your mouth. Try to warm the air before it goes into your lungs. That oughta help."

The Cereal Tycoon

*   *   *

It was now almost five years since Anna and Luther had arrived in Cleveland. Young Henry Parsons Crowell grew up in the small house at 14 Sheriff Street and enjoyed its comforts.

Little Harry, as his parents called him, began life in the nursery on the second floor of the home. He was too young to be aware of his father's growing business success or the skills and acumen which permitted Luther to make money. But Harry's parents were quite conscious of how God was blessing them. In addition to the nursery, rare for most homes, their house had other rooms that in that day seemed to be superfluous--a double parlor, twice the size of those of ordinary houses, plus extra bedrooms and even a dining room.

Anna took good care of the home, her touch being quite evident. Small pieces of Early American glass gleamed like jewels in the sunny bay windows. Paintings graced the walls of the parlor and other rooms. Embroidered samplers and painted mottoes, beautifully framed and placed in prominent places, were reminders of God's goodness and gave inspiration to those who were invited to the home for tea or an elegant dinner.

In plain sight on the dining room buffet was the big family Bible. No meal was ever eaten without this book. Luther would read a passage from it, perhaps offer simple comments of application, then lead the family in prayer. Young Harry prayed too, but sometimes his eyes were open ever so slightly to see what Mama had put on the table that smelled so good during Papa's prayers.

After dinner most nights, the boy was put to bed, this time with Mama's prayers, and after he was tucked in, Anna went downstairs where she and Luther talked about the day's events and planned for their future. It was during one of these talks that Anna sensed a seriousness in her husband.

"Is something wrong?" she asked him.

Luther shook his head. "Not really. In fact, just the opposite. I can't get over the way things are going for us. We have more money now than I ever dreamed of making."

Anna smiled in relief. "You mean that you miss the days when we had less?"

Her husband laughed. He was silent for a moment, then the serious expression on his face returned. "Anna, I feel a sense of responsibility for our good fortune. Do you remember what Dr. Eells said in his sermon Sunday?"

"You mean the Bible verse about the person who has been given much--that much will be required of him?"

"Yes, exactly." Luther replied. "I was thinking about stewardship. Money. I've seen what unusual wealth can sometimes do to people. It seems especially true out here on the frontier. Some people get away from their roots, family and church and they seem to forget God. There are a lot of people like us who have prospered by coming west. A lot of them don't think much about God. And the next generation doesn't quite know how to handle it. I'm concerned about Harry . . . and any other children we might have. I don't want them to have parents who let money take the place of God. Or, be spoiled by wealth."

Anna wasn't sure she fully understood all of his concern. As if reading her mind, he explained his fears. "Anna, you've seen it, too. Some families with wealth turn it over to their children when they die and there are all sorts of troubles because of money. I'm going to pray that God will give us wisdom to help our children know how to use wealth and not the other way around."

The next day, Luther Crowell thought more about the conversation with his wife the night before. Of course, he had not told his wife what had prompted his concern for their future. But she would soon understand.

It was June, and flowers were abundant in the gardens and lanes. The weather was unseasonably warm and sunny, with the sounds of children playing. Luther had just come from a meeting with his partner, John Seymour, where the two of them had discussed their business.

Luther offered some changes for their partnership agreement that allowed for either partner to handle the problems of succession in the event something happened to either one of them. Luther took these signed agreements, put them into a leather folder and told Seymour that he'd deliver them to their attorney after lunch.

Lunch was eaten at home, with his family. Young Harry asked his father, after eating, if he might go back to the shoe store with him and help. Luther smiled. "In time, son. You go out and play now. You'll have time for work later." He kissed Anna and headed back toward town. It was true that he was stopping at the attorney's office. But there was another appointment he'd scheduled that neither his partner nor wife knew about.

Outside the offices of their family doctor, Luther paused for an instant, then walked up the wooden steps to the small foyer. By coming just after lunch, Dr. Naught had assured Luther he wouldn't have to wait in the usually crowded waiting room.

Sitting on the edge of the examining table, Luther was silent as the doctor listened to his chest. Then Dr. Naught was finished. "You can put your shirt back on," he said. As Luther dressed, he already knew the answer.

"I've had lung trouble most all of my life," he confided to Dr. Naught. "But this is the first year I can remember having it this late in the year."

The doctor nodded. "Your lungs are filled. And your blood's been affected. That's what saps your strength. You need rest. Real rest."

"Maybe I'll take Harry and Anna and take a holiday. We could journey down the Ohio on a steamer."

"The fresh air ought to help. But . . . ."

Luther saw a dark expression on Dr. Naught's face.

"What is it?"

"Well, Luther, you've got tuberculosis. That's a fancy name for what we've always called consumption. And I think you already know there's no cure. The newspapers say that big American cities--like New York, Boston, and Philadelphia--have the highest rates in the world. TB's the biggest cause of death in these cities. Sure, we're learning more about tuberculosis, and one day there might--"

"I know," Luther sighed. "I'm resigned to it."

The diagnosis was not a surprise, but Luther had hoped he'd escape this death sentence. "How much time do I have?"

"It's hard to say. Maybe a couple years, even five. Probably not that much, though. Sorry, Luther."

Dr. Naught had merely confirmed Luther's suspicions. At 35 he should be in the prime of life, but instead, he was pale, anemic and had been losing weight consistently. The winter's hacking cough still hung on in June, long after he'd lost it in previous years.

Consumption, or tuberculosis, robbed its victims of hope as well as health. It preyed on the young; many never even got to finish childhood. Fathers with babies should have qualified for a reprieve, but there was no such luck.

"You'll have to tell Anna," Dr. Naught said.

"I suppose so," Luther acknowledged. "Can you help me? Will you come over for dinner and explain it to her?"

The doctor nodded. Although it was the same as issuing a death sentence, Dr. Naught had real experience in telling people about dying. His calm and reassuring manner could ease the emotional impact of such a pronouncement to the young wife, but nothing could really make it easy.

* * * *

Little Harry didn't really know what his father was experiencing. Despite the hopelessness of Luther's future, immediate days were spent carefully, as if time was as much of the family's treasure as money. Work and family were Luther's total preoccupations now. He built up his prosperous business even more, and added to his family.

A brother for Harry was born on New Year's day, 1861. Harry was now six and his parents named the new baby Edward.

Two years later, another brother, Charles was born.

In addition to the fact that all three were boys, there was something else that they all had in common. Each boy--Harry, Edward and Charles--had inherited Luther's genetic constitution. All three would later contract the same dreaded tuberculosis. Two of them, Edward and Charles, would die from it. Only Harry would survive.

Luther did not know that now, of course, but he began to plan for its possibility. The disease was well known to make an appearance in successive generations. Acutely aware of his own limited time, he took conscious efforts to make plans not only for his own absence from the family, but to cover needs not yet known.

He had twin concerns. The first he had discussed with Anna on that June evening several years earlier. He wanted to set the example by making God central to his life and that of each family member. The second issue had to do with providing for his family after he was gone. There was an overlapping consideration that brought the two together.

As a young man in Connecticut, Luther had seen that wealth kept for two or three generations could corrupt those who were inexperienced with it. He saw the same thing happen in Cleveland.

"Wealth will either poison its possessor or be a tool for great accomplishment," Luther told his new pastor. Dr. Theron Hawks had succeeded Luther's friend, Dr. Eells, as minister of the Second Presbyterian Church (where the Crowell family

17

attended). Dr. Hawks listened to Luther express his concerns. "The Bible is clear about the choices involved in serving God or mammon. It's quite hard to keep money from being your god," the minister commented.

"That's what I mean. I've seen it too often," replied Luther. "When money is earned apart from God, or if it's kept without Him, it's the children who grow up into that wealth who are destroyed."

"I think I know what you're saying," Dr. Hawks observed. "The Bible says, *'A fool and his money are soon parted.'* And, *'A man cannot serve two masters'* --he must serve God or mammon."

"That's true," said Luther. "But what I'm saying is that God must be involved from the beginning--with the making and using of money. I think that's the reason God blesses our family. We've made Him the head of our house, and we exercise the stewardship of tithing."

The pastor nodded agreement. "By asking for God's wisdom in the acquisition of material things, those things are put into perspective."

"And in the case of illness, money can buy doctors, and nurses," Luther continued. "It can buy education and housing, meals and clothes when I'm not here to see to it."

Luther did not want his home to lose its God-centric basis and he prayed it would always be so. Otherwise money would be lavished on selfishness and sinfulness. He'd also seen how deep into debauchery a man (or woman, for that matter) could sink with the help of riches.

The ailing father set about to make certain that his young family would stay true to the right use of wealth. He created a trust for his family that would leave them with enough money to keep them in the style of living that he'd been providing for them. Then, there was money set aside for schooling. And upon becoming adults, money would be there to help the children start out on their own.

Yet, there were strings attached. The trust saw to it that there was no way for immature or selfish children to get hold of money when it might do them harm. Anna would be taken care of, too. And the business could continue. He'd thought of everything.

*　　*　　*　　*

Luther continued to work in his business but grew steadily weaker. The Civil War had started and was being waged during these years. He'd escaped the draft because of his consumption yet devoted himself to the war effort by making boots for Union soldiers. This effort only added to the success of his already thriving business.

In his fortieth year, Luther's illness grew much worse. He was now bedridden nearly all of the time. Anna nursed him through the difficulty. Harry, now nine, even tried to help look after his father.

"Papa," asked Harry, "do you think you'll feel better by Christmas?"

"Well, son," Luther replied, "let's hope so."

Anna came into the room, wiped Luther's forehead and suggested to Harry, "Why not read to your father?"

"All right!" The youngster's eyes brightened. He welcomed the chance to show off his reading skills. "What should I read to you, Papa?"

"I'd like to hear you read from the Bible. The Psalms. Or is that too difficult for you?"

"No, sir. I can do that!" Harry ran downstairs to get the family Bible from the dining room. He was back in less than a minute, leafing through the heavy book to find a text.

"Read from the 23rd Psalm," his father requested. Harry found that passage and began to read, sounding out phonetically the bigger words with which he wasn't quite as familiar. "He leadeth me in the paths of *right-e-ous-ness* for His name's sake. Yea, though I walk through the valley of the *sha-dow* of death, I will fear no evil . . . ."

The young voice was clear and the words reassuring. Harry read the familiar passage and some others that his mother helped him find. Soon his father was sleeping.

The next day, November 20, 1864, Harry's Uncle Will came over to the house. After a brief talk with Harry's mother, Uncle Will took the boy downstairs and put on his coat. Then he took Harry hurriedly away from the house. Harry doesn't remember much more about that day, except later he was told that his father had died. Luther Crowell had lost his on-going, life-long battle with tuberculosis.

*   *   *   *

None of Luther's three sons really grasped the significance of his death. The undertaker had come and carried away their father in a wagon but not in their sight. They only knew that somehow, somewhat suddenly, he was gone. They were told he had died and was now in heaven, but they were confused and frightened.

A number of relatives and friends dropped by the house over the next several days. Harry saw his mother weeping. His brothers went over to hold onto her apron or hug her. Harry wished he could comfort his mother and ease her terrible pain.

At the church, a memorial service took place, followed by a graveside burial at the cemetery. The weather had turned bleak and a raw, gusty wind made Harry shiver as he watched them lower the wooden coffin into the ground.

Strangely, during these days, Harry suddenly grew up. Uncle Will, his mother's sister's husband, had told Harry that as the eldest son, now he was the "man" of the family. The boy knew he couldn't fill his father's shoes--work in the shoe business, take care of the house, pay the bills. Is that what he was supposed to do now as the man in the family? Harry wondered what Uncle Will meant, especially since he'd already heard him tell Mama, "Remember Anna, if there's anything at all you need, just let us know."

The nine-year-old suddenly felt relieved that his aunt and uncle would be there if they needed help.

Later, young Harry listened when Dr. Hawks came around to offer heartfelt and sympathetic consolation. His words were comforting, and he seemed to understand what had happened. In the memorial service, the preacher told of his conversations with Luther--how the devout husband and father had sought God's will for his life and his family. He spoke of Luther's quest for faith as the search for the "pearl of great price". Harry knew the parable, having recently read about it in the Bible. Dr. Hawks also talked about the father's concern to have right priorities for his business and finances.

"But perhaps the most important matter in Luther's life was his relationship with Jesus Christ. Nothing to him was as great as being a Christian with a servant's heart," the pastor told those in the pews.

Harry listened and thought much about his father, about his faith, and of his journey to heaven from his sickbed. There was much the boy did not fully understand, but his mind was beginning to put the matters into focus. It was all overwhelming. At the grave of his father, Harry began to sob. At the conclusion of the service, the minister once more came over to console the family.

Stopping in front of Anna at graveside, Dr. Hawks took her hand and bowed his head. He prayed with her in a voice not louder than a whisper, words meant to encourage the grieving wife and mother. They were the words Anna needed to hear, and she smiled despite her tears as the minister concluded the prayer.

Next, Dr. Hawks patted the heads of the two younger boys. However, turning to Harry, he shook hands with him, granting him stature over his brothers. Harry's tiny fingers were enveloped by the huge hand of the pastor. He felt its warmth and gentle pressure. Looking up, Harry, still crying, blurted, "Dr. Hawks, may I come and see you tomorrow?"

"Of course, son. Come to the church. I'll be in my study after nine."

That night, Harry tossed and turned in his bed. The events of the past several days had caught up with him, and he was emotionally wrung out and still very much in fear of what had taken place. He cried softly into his pillow and eventually fell asleep.

The next morning, he went to Dr. Hawk's study. The minister was seated at a huge and imposing desk, with books and papers scattered about. At the boy's soft knock, he looked up and smiled. "Come in, lad. Please . . . have a seat." He pointed to the large leather chair directly across from his desk.

Harry crawled up into the chair and squirmed to be comfortable, but his feet did not reach the floor. The minister rose and walked over to a nearby *settee* and fetched a small footstool placed nearby. He carried it over and put it under Harry's feet.

"What brings you to visit me?" Dr. Hawks asked.

"Well, sir," Harry stammered, "I . . . I--uh--" Frustrated by his inability to articulate his thoughts, the boy started to get up. The minister gestured for him to stay.

"It's all right, Harry. I know you're going through difficult times just now. You're afraid, and sad. Maybe even a little bit angry that your father has left you, eh?"

Harry looked up, surprised. How did he know? And was it all right to feel angry at such a time? In a moment or so, Harry finally found words. He talked about being afraid, angry, confused. But more than anything, he wanted to talk to Dr. Hawks about his father's faith.

22

"How come Papa is in heaven? Why did he die? What happens when you die? When will I die? What happens if my Mama dies?" The questions came as a volley.

The minister smiled reassuringly. "You have a lot on your mind for a young lad. But I sense that you have some thoughts that are far beyond your years. And what is it that troubles you most?"

The boy sank back into the leather chair. He felt helpless again, and small. "I . . . I guess that what upsets me most is whether I can go to heaven and see my father. How do you get to go to heaven, sir?"

"Well, young man," the minister smiled, "of all the questions you could have asked, that is probably the one I can answer with the most authority. You see, I'm an expert on heaven. It's my job to tell people how to go to heaven."

For nearly an hour the pastor and his youthful inquirer talked. Harry heard what the minister called "the Good News" and how to become a Christian--something to be settled in his mind and heart. He explained things to Harry in words the boy could understand. He didn't use the theological terms or ecclesiastical expressions that brought confusion. Instead, he shared these thoughts with simplicity and sensitivity and introduced Harry to Jesus, God's Son.

And the young seeker understood. He bowed his head and prayed with the minister, inviting Jesus to come into his life and show him the way to live for God. In all the years to follow, this experience would never be forgotten, nor would its reality ever leave Harry. When he got up from the huge chair to leave, he was conscious of something wonderful having taken place within him. The power, validity and wonder of that event would be ever-present in Harry's life and work and stay with him for the rest of his earthly life.

Chapter Two

Following the death of Luther Crowell, Anna's brother, Joel Parsons, moved from Connecticut to live with the fatherless family. He was 34, and had been asked by Luther before he died to be guardian of the boys. Later, Joel married and brought his new bride to live with the Crowell family in Cleveland.

But in a real sense, no one could take Luther's place. Of course, Uncle Joel and his wife were a great help to the family, but it was Luther's widow, Anna, who did the most remarkable job in maintaining the values and ideals that Luther had established in their Christian home. He had also left Anna with enough funds to allow the family to live comfortably. Anna also continued the tradition of devotions and Bible reading, church attendance, faith and obedience.

During the first years following his father's death, Harry had come to appreciate Dr. Hawks' occasional chats and encouragement. He also loved and appreciated Uncle Joel, with whom he bonded as a surrogate father.

Harry had learned to read and write from his mother. Uncle Joel taught him about history, politics and current events. During these grim days of the Civil War, Uncle Joel had told him the meaning behind the terrible newspaper headlines. His uncle also gave him history books and biographies to read, but in matters of faith, he was tutored by his mother and his pastor, Dr. Hawks. As Harry studied for his confirmation in the Presbyterian Church, he read the Bible and books about the early martyrs. *Pilgrim's Progress* and other classics were also introduced to him and they left a mark on his consciousness.

These three teachers--his mother, Uncle Joel and Dr. Hawks--impressed upon him the importance of education. They even had consensus as to where he might find the best instruction. Yale University, the unfulfilled dream of his father, was laid out before Harry as *his* destiny.

It was at this impressionable age that the boy was introduced to the sermons of a travelling revivalist. Charles G. Finney, a lawyer turned preacher, was also president of Oberlin College. His messages featured a daring and powerful method of evangelism. After a clear sermon on sin and salvation, Finney invited his hearers who became convicted of their sins, to come to the front of the church and kneel at an "anxious bench" where they could pray for forgiveness and salvation.

Finney had an optimistic view of redeemed man, and he encouraged seekers to first become Christians, then--as believers--they should work on behalf of God, not to earn their salvation, but as an expression of their gratitude to Him for their salvation.

Harry Crowell had already given his heart and life to Christ as a nine-year-old boy in Dr. Hawks' study three years earlier. Now, he prayed that God would use his talents and abilities for His kingdom. He wanted to make his life count for something--something significant. This boy, a serious and thoughtful Christian, seemed wise beyond his years. He knew from hearing the reports of Uncle Joel, Dr. Hawks and others, that the Civil War would end soon.

Harry believed that this was of those who had acted on Finney's call to action, and because so many were praying for God to intervene. He *would* answer their prayers and make an end to the suffering.

So then, Harry sought a personal objective--some goal that would give his own life significance. *But what?*

*　　　*　　　*　　　*

In 1865 the Civil War ended. In addition to the loss of President Lincoln, the Union lost 360,000 men--husbands, fathers, brothers, sons. The Confederacy fared no better with 258,000 killed. Nearly a half-million more were wounded or maimed on both sides. It would take generations for America to mend itself after this horrible war.

And as if the Civil War wasn't enough, during these years, a worldwide cholera epidemic also struck around the world. Thousands died in dozens of cities. In September, 1865, some *200 people a day* perished in Paris. In Austria, 110,000 died. Even more fatalities were recorded in Prussia. America lost 50,000 to cholera. Cleveland was not spared from the plague, but somehow the Crowell home was safe and the death angel bypassed the family.

By 1867, America began to rebuild. Harry, now 12, took a job in the shoe business that his father had founded, now being run by Luther's former partner. Mr. Childs was kind and treated Harry as his own son. Young Crowell was growing taller and already had the build of a young man. Harry learned the business quickly. The other workers were older, and had learned shoe manufacturing when shoes were mostly handmade. Harry's father, on the other hand, had early embraced the benefits of new technology. His workers at first may have secretly worried that a new-fangled machine would take away their jobs, but Luther had shown them that machines could do just the opposite--creating new jobs, and less tedious ones at that.

Harry never had any experience with the old ways of doing things, so he didn't have to overcome any resistance to the new technology. While others fought the new technologies, the new ways of doing things, Harry understood from the start how such innovations could be beneficial. He was not yet in his teens, but here he was, suggesting new methods and procedures for improving the manufacture or marketing of shoes.

His employer confided in Harry one day. "Son, what are your plans for the future? Have you considered coming into the business?"

"Uh . . . no I haven't, Mr. Childs. I know that my father was successful in it, and he made a good living. But my family wants me to go to Yale. And, Papa--uh, my father--wanted to go to Yale, but never could because of his health.," Harry replied.

"Do you have any particular calling, son? I mean like a lawyer, or a clergyman . . . maybe an educator?"

"No, sir, not really. But Uncle Joel--he's my guardian--says with all the changes in the world, a man will never make anything of himself unless he's educated. He wants me to go to Yale. And so does my mother."

"I see. Well, you've got time to think about it. Who knows, maybe you'll change your mind and come to work with me. You've got a real head for business."

Harry did work in the shoe business during summer vacations. But in the summer of 1867, his boyhood friend, Howard Eells (son of the minister who was Luther's close friend) came to see him, having just finished his freshman year at a preparatory school. Harry and his mother had talked about what prep school Harry would go toin order to prepare for Yale, but no choice had been made.

The boys were inseparable that summer. Whenever he could get off work, Harry went fishing with Howard. Or they'd play baseball. Invariably, during their times together, Howard would sell his friend on the many merits of the Greylock Institute. To Harry, it all sounded exotic. Greylock Institute was far away in Massachusetts. You had to travel by train all night and all day just to get there!

Howard described every detail of the place--how the building sat surrounded by the mountains of the Berkshire Hills, in the shadow of Mount Greylock. He told about the oak and maple trees turning red in the fall, the pond freezing over, the enthusiasm of the boys at Greylock toward everything except schooling.

Harry laughed. "What about sports?" he asked. "You know how I like sports."

It was the opening Howard was waiting for. "Sports? Greylock has the best. The finest players in all of Massachusetts. Really! Baseball, tennis, everything. Why, we even have winter sports like skating, bobsleds, toboggans. Summer and winter. We play all the time."

"Don't you ever study?"

"Well, of course. But a person's got to have other interests, too, y'know!"

"What about fishing?"

"That, too." Howard grinned. "There's all kinds of creeks and streams comin' down from the mountains. And they're full of trout--big, speckled brown beauties this big." He held out his arms in front of him, slowly pulling his hands apart to show the length of the fish, growing spectacularly as he told his tale.

Both of them laughed. The conversations continued throughout the summer vacation. Because both boys had been touched by the Finney revivals, each had an earnest desire to serve Christ. As the summer slid by, their conversations became more serious. Howard talked about the teachers, Bible instruction and most important to him, the school's president.

"Dr. Mills is really great," Howard told Harry. "He understands us. He knows what we're thinking at this age in our lives. He encourages us without hitting us over the head with a sermon. Y'know what I mean?"

It didn't take many more of Howard's sales pitches to convince Harry. One afternoon he went to Uncle Joel to talk about going to school at the Greylock Institute. Harry, until now, had led a fairly sheltered life as to finances. He had no idea what it would cost, although he had saved much of the salary he'd earned working at *Crowell & Childs.*

"So you want me to help you convince your mother to let you go to Greylock? And you want to know if you have enough money to go to school?" Uncle Joel asked.

"Yes, sir. I'll need money for books, tuition and such. Then there's meals and lodging. And the cost of the train trip to Massachusetts. I've got enough saved up from working for the first year," Harry explained. He showed his uncle a printed brochure telling of the school. *Greylock Institute is the Select Family School for Boys,* the headline stated.

Harry pointed to the page with financial information. "It says for room and board, washing clothes, mending, use of the school library, bed and bedding costs $450 a year. And it's an extra $6 for the winter term if we want a stove to heat our room. I figure with other expenses it'll come to $500 a year. But I'm not sure about the years after that. I mean, there's all the years at Greylock, then there's Yale, and I don't even know how much that'll cost."

Uncle Joel smiled. "Harry," he said softly, "sit down."

Harry did as he was told.

"As you know," he began, "your father appointed me your guardian, to help your mother."

Harry nodded.

"Well, Harry, your father was a wise and prudent man. He made good money while he was alive and was a good steward of it. Even though he gave a great deal of it to church causes, there was still a lot left over. Your father invested it. Then he established a trust for your mother so there'd be enough money for her to live on and take care of you boys."

"Yes, sir," Harry nodded. "But is there enough to help with my schooling? I mean, I'll work summers and maybe find a job near the school to help. I can't take the money that Mother needs. But--"

"There's no need, son. Your father left you an inheritance."

"Inheritance?" Harry asked.

"Yes. He left you $27,000."

Harry's eyes widened. In 1867, that kind of money was a fortune.

"With good management that money will not only take care of all your school expenses, but there'll be enough left over to help you get started in life," his uncle explained.

"I--I don't know what to say," whispered Harry. Amazed at his father's foresight and prudence, Harry sat for a long moment reflecting over his uncle's words.

"It's your money, son. You can use it for school."

"But it's not mine, Uncle Joel. It's my father's. He earned it. He saved it. Maybe he set it aside for me. But it's still his money. Or rather, it's *the Lord's*. It's a huge amount of money. Sir, I believe I'm obliged to be careful with it."

Uncle Joel smiled his approval. Harry continued, "Father's been gone for three years now, but I do remember his ways. He used to tell me about stewardship when I was little. When I put my pennies in the collection at church, he'd say, *'Handling money is a holy trust, Harry. Stewardship is something you've got to take seriously'.*"

"He was right, son," Uncle Joel replied. "One of the reasons your father asked me to be your guardian was that he'd seen too many lives wrecked by the inability to handle money. Harry, your father wanted you to remember God as you use this money. Don't let it run through your fingers like sand. Be a wise and careful steward."

Harry's sincere expression and response had shown Uncle Joel that his words had made the right impression upon his nephew. "What are you thinking?" he asked Harry.

Harry paused before he answered. Then his eyes shown with a wisdom beyond his years. "I was just thinking about that verse in the Bible, you know--the one that says 'Before you ask I will answer'? Well, I've been worried about how I'd get enough money to get me all through school. But I knew it was God's will that I go on with my education. So when I made up my mind to go off to school, I prayed about it. But He was ahead of me. God put it in my father's heart to take care of me, of my education, even before I asked."

"Yes, Harry. It's good that you have these wonderful memories of your father. Most boys would be grateful for a father with such provision. But you're a wise son indeed to recognize your *heavenly* Father in all of this. Not many lads are wise enough, mature enough, to see that. I'd venture to say that you'll do very well by following this path. Yes, *very well indeed!"*

*   *   *   *

Howard Eells and Harry Crowell entered Greylock Institute in the fall of 1867. Harry had never before been away from home for any length of time, so for awhile he was a bit homesick. But soon he was so involved with the activities that he was distracted about how much he missed his family and Cleveland. He wrote to his mother and Uncle Joel frequently, and their letters to him were small treasures from home that he looked forward to with pleasure.

Greylock Institute had over a thousand students in attendance. All were expected to act as gentlemen, do their classwork and behave. Any truancies were immediately reported to parents, as were any failures in daily recitations or poor grades. All students were expected to be in church on Sunday. And, no one questioned these rules. It was expected of all young men who were serious about life and education.

Still, Greylock was not an austere place. Its president, Benjamin Franklin Mills, had started the school 25 years earlier. His was an unusual incorporation. As a young man, he had just come from the farm and had been a clerk in the store. He was asked to go into partnership with another man who, through mismanagement, ran up huge debts and the business failed. The failure left Mills in heavy indebtedness, but with a sense of moral obligation to repay the debts.

But by the time he earned enough to pay off the creditors, it was too late for him to go to college. His dreams died; he'd go through life without a formal college education. But Mills chose not to wallow in self-pity. He took on the challenge and purpose of starting a school to help *others* get an education, even if he could not. He personally financed costs of land and building and the Greylock Institute became a reality.

His moral strength, character and crusader's purpose became the model for his students. They looked up to Mills and he repaid their respect in kind. He showed individual attention to each student--trying to learn each of their names and taking a personal interest in each life.

Harry admired the president to the point of real affection. After the loss of his father, Benjamin Mills took his place. The president was a man of authority, but also a gentle man. He listened intently to the questions and problems of "his boys" and tried to assess the real reasons behind their words. Finally, the boy would ask, "What would *you* do, Mr. Mills?"

"Just take your time, son. Be sure to find the will of God, then do it," was often his simple reply. Young Crowell made this a personal credo in those early school years: *Take your time . . . and find the will of God.*

In such a fine setting as Greylock, Harry made unusual progress. As the months passed, he applied himself to his studies. Actually, he enjoyed athletics and shined in these efforts. He was a natural talent in tennis and baseball; literature and math required more effort. Yet, all in all, Harry was a normal American boy.

In his thirteenth year, starting with his birthday in January, Harry was becoming a young man. His voice had changed; he was taller, and his studies reflected a serious interest in doing what was expected of him.

His mother could not believe her eyes when he got off the train as school let out for the summer. She breathed a sigh of relief when she saw how healthy he seemed--remembering Harry's lingering cough the winter before he left for school. Anna did not ask him if he'd had a bad cough this past winter, but she knew he was his father's son. One day, he would also have to contend with "lung trouble".

Chapter Three

Greylock had become Harry Crowell's real home during most of the past four years. It was 1872, and he was a serious student of 17 preparing for Yale. It would take five years of study, but by next year, God willing, he'd be ready.

During the winter of 1871-72, Harry began to suffer with the strain of that lingering cough that both he and his mother feared. He remembered very little of his father--his face was by now just a memory. But he recalled vividly the uncontrollable spasms of coughing of his father just before he died. The Massachusetts winters were often less harsh than those in Cleveland, yet Harry's winter illnesses seemed to be getting worse.

By April, Harry was feeling much better. Then, in the midst of classes, a tragedy occurred. A fire started on the Greylock grounds. Before anyone could do anything about it, the school burned to the ground. Everyone was devastated although no lives were lost.

President Mills brought all the students together and tried to reassure them. He vowed to rebuild Greylock as soon as possible. "We'll have to dismiss you now. You can go back home with an early summer recess. But be prepared to return in the fall! I'll find the money, somehow, and I'll rebuild Greylock--right here where it stood before. You'll see. Come back in the fall and we'll resume school, just as if nothing had ever happened!"

Harry took the train back to Cleveland and returned to working in the shoe business while he waited. In the fall, just before the start of school, he went to see Dr. Naught for a check-up. The family physician took his time and gave Harry a thorough examination.

Dr. Naught suddenly felt ill himself. There was a feeling of *deja vu* as he told young Crowell to put his shirt back on. While Harry was dressing, the doctor excused himself and went into the other room where Anna was waiting. He saw the apprehension in her eyes and wished he could offer an answer to sweep it away.

"I'm sorry, Anna. You were right. He's not getting any better. In fact, Harry will have to drop out of school--"

"*No!*" Anna cried.

"--he'll have to drop out of school or die," the doctor added. "Harry has lung trouble, same as Luther. He's going to have to quit school and take care of himself." Dr. Naught watched helplessly as Anna's shoulders fell and she began to sob. He excused himself and walked back to the other room.

Harry was devastated when Dr. Naught came back and told him the same news. "But I can't drop out now," he pleaded. "I've only got one more year 'til graduation from Greylock. I need that in order to get into Yale."

Dr. Naught sighed deeply. "I'm sorry, son. If you don't drop out now, you'll die."

His bluntness finally captured Harry's attention. "All right. I guess I can take a year off, maybe get some private tutoring and keep up that way then graduate with the rest of my class next year."

The physician shook his head. "You don't understand how sick you are, Harry. You can't make *any* long term plans just now."

Long term plans. Harry heard the words and ran them over in his mind. Often at school, or at work, he'd think about the future. It was easy to lay it all out in strict linear fashion-- plans for five years at Greylock, another four at Yale. Then? Could he really plan nine or ten years out? If he'd inherited his father's illness, perhaps ten years might be all he had. His thoughts went to the grass-covered grave in Woodland Cemetery where his father was buried. Was that to be his lot as well? Ten years.

Finally he asked, "Does my mother know?"

The doctor nodded. "She knows. She's been worried about it for several years. When your cough didn't clear up last spring, she suspected the worst. She saw the same thing happening to you that happened to your father. So she's rightfully scared."

Harry's concern for himself was overshadowed by his feelings for his mother. He went to her. Anna put her arms around her son and began to weep quietly.

"It'll be all right, Mother," he said.

Soon Anna recovered her composure. She went to get her coat. Harry turned to the doctor. "How long do I have?" he asked.

"Well, son, the bad news is, I don't know. The good news is, medicine's been making good progress since your father's illness. Some doctors learned that making patients take lots of rest, sending them to a better climate and getting them into the outdoors, the disease might be checked."

"You mean there's a cure?"

"Well, I can't say that exactly. They don't know yet. But it's the only answer we've got today. I know this--if you *don't* drop out of school and get good rest, you'll die. That much I know for sure."

Harry's mother came back into the room. "Mrs. Crowell," Dr. Naught said to her, "Please don't give up hope.

There's some good news in all of this." He told her what he'd just shared with Harry.

Then he turned again to Harry, explaining, "You'll have to spend seven, eight--maybe even ten years recovering your health. I know it's a long time. But there's no other way."

*   *   *   *

Dr. Naught was asked by Harry if it was all right if he worked at the *Crowell & Childs* shoe firm. The doctor seemed to think this activity might be good for him, take his mind off his illness and missing school. So Harry continued working as a clerk, but not as a restful activity. He worked every bit as hard as any of the other clerks.

The autumn months and winter passed without too much difficulty. Missing the daily discipline of devotions and Bible study at Greylock, Harry began to seriously read the Bible on his own.

His Bible study impressed upon Harry that there was great significance in the tithe. He counted out a tenth of his income and brought it to church every Sunday. It was a lesson learned soundly and the habit would be forever with him. Learning to give God his portion when earning only hundreds of dollars a year set the pattern for his future when his income would rise to over a million dollars a year.

There was another event that would leave its mark on the young man. It was spring, 1873, and Harry was eighteen. There was a special meeting at the Second Presbyterian Church in Cleveland. A fiery businessman turned evangelist had been invited to speak. He was mostly unpolished and a self-educated man but he had a dynamic message.

His name was Dwight Lyman Moody, originally from New England, now from Chicago. Moody told the congregation that his heart was on fire to get to Great Britain and preach.

"Now most of you know that I planned to be in Liverpool, England," Moody told his audience. "The churches there sent me an invitation to come. They said they'd follow it up with money for travel. But so far, it ain't come. So, when your pastor extended me the invitation to come to Cleveland, I didn't have a good reason to turn him down. So here I am!" Moody's speech was down to earth but filled with passion.

As Harry thought of the well-crafted and sonorous words of his school president, Benjamin Mills, Moody seemed rough-hewn and plain. But, like Mr. Mills, Moody's words hung in the air in the front of Harry's mind then pounced inside for effect. Harry couldn't take his eyes off the evangelist.

"Now, I want ya to know," Moody said loudly, "that I like to think big things for God! Do you? Fr'instance, I wanna go to England and win ten thousand souls. Can ya imagine? Why that's a thousand times more people than what's here tonight. Think of it." He paused to let his words sink in.

"And what about you?" Moody's gaze, as well as his words, seemed directed exactly at Harry. He caught his breath and listened.

"That's right. What about you? Do *you* ever think big things for God? Huh?"

The big room was absolutely silent, save for a single muffled cough or two.

Harry rolled the thought over in his mind. . . . *ever think big things for God?*

Moody continued. "The reason I like to think big things for God is that He deserves it. Now, whether it's evangelism, or your work, or your money. Whatever it is, you ought to think of big ways you can be used for God. Now let me tell you 'bout a feller I met in Ireland."

Harry's gaze and attention were firmly fixed on the speaker. Moody was not terribly tall, but his heavy-set frame made him seem more imposing. His dark beard moved up and down, and his arms were animated as he spoke.

"That feller I met in Ireland was Henry Varley. Lemme tell you what he told me. Varley sez t'me, ' *The world has yet to see what God can do with and for and through and in a man who is fully and wholly consecrated to Him'.*"

Moody repeated the sentence for emphasis. "Now listen," he cried out. "That was like the Word of God to my soul. Those words pierced my heart. *Listen!* The world has yet to see . . . what God can do *with* a man . . . and what God can do *for* a man. And what God can do *through* and *in* a man. A *man.* And Varley meant *any man!* He didn't say he had to be educated."

The words again seemed directed to Harry.

The evangelist continued, hammering the air for emphasis. "Varley didn't say he had to be brilliant, or rich, or anything else. A *man.* Just *a man!* Well, I told God, that with the Holy Spirit in me, *I'll* be that man. And what about you? Will you be one of those men? Is your God worthy of such a commitment?"

Harry Crowell could not hold back his tears. He put his face into his hands, bowing his head on the back of the pew in front of him, sunk low in submission. Moody's voice reinforced Harry's conviction that God was speaking directly to him.

"That's why I want to dream great things for God," the evangelist said. "I want to get back to England and win ten thousand souls for the Savior. And what about you? What great thing will you do? Remember, Varley said, 'A man. *Any man.*' Will you be such a man?"

The evangelist sat down at the front of the church as the pastor concluded the service in prayer. Harry was so powerfully affected that he slipped quietly outside. Walking away from the church, he heard the people singing a hymn.

He walked slowly along the lake shore, lost in thought for some time, watching the water and listening to its gentle lapping. After awhile, Harry sat down on a large rock, still shaken by Moody's words.

God, Harry prayed silently, *there is no mistaking that these have been Your words to me. I can see that You can use me even if I must leave school. Mr. Moody said I don't have to be an educated man, or brilliant, or anything. Just a man. Lord, by Your grace and with the help of the Holy Spirit, I'll be that man.*

Still deep in meditation, Harry thought about what he might do for God. What kind of *big dreams* should he have in the service of God? *I know I can never preach like Mr. Moody . . . but maybe I can do something else great for You. Lord, maybe I can make money and help support men like D. L. Moody.*

The thought was there, but how did it get there? As Harry reflected, he knew this was something he wanted to do for God. This would be his dream, a dream of great things for the Lord. But then, Varley's words to Moody came back to Harry-- *a man who is fully and wholly consecrated to Him.*

Harry knew that part was as important as the first part concerning availability.

He continued in prayer. *Oh, God . . . if You will allow me to make money, to be used for Your service, I'll keep my name out of it. I'll do it so You will get the glory.*

This was his sincere commitment; Harry meant it. This purposeful prayer and subsequent resolve to make money for the Lord's service was sealed, a commitment which eventually enabled God to entrust millions of dollars with Harry.

As Harry walked back to the church, the service was over. The people had been dismissed, and Moody was gone. Harry wanted to shake his hand and thank him for the powerful message that God brought to young Crowell through the evangelist. But he was not there. And Harry would never see Moody again.

The Cereal Tycoon

*   *   *   *

A full year went by after Moody's visit to the Cleveland church where Harry Crowell heard him and had made his decisive commitment to make money with God's help. But Harry's health declined badly, almost at inverse proportion to his spiritual growth.

Harry could no longer work at *Crowell & Childs*, and was almost constantly bedridden. During his imposed rests, Harry grew more and more involved in the Bible. He wrote letters and notes to friends and associates, encouraging them and telling them of God. He was not depressed at his sickness and its attendant handicap of being bedridden. Somehow, he never took his disease as fatal. The doctor had told him that seven to ten years of rest might help him, so Harry was resigned to spending this time in bed. He made the most of it by reading and Bible study.

One aspect of his study fascinated him. He was struck by how often the Bible referred to the number seven. The Spirit specified *seven men of honest report* (Acts 6:3); the prophet built *seven altars* and was able to gain the ear of God (Numbers 23:14); to *go wash in the Jordan River seven times* (2 Kings 5:10) and many others. *Seven baskets. Seven candlesticks. Seven weeks, seven maidens, seven cubits.* The number seven had significance in the Bible.

During one such time in the study of the Scriptures, Harry came upon a verse that really struck him. Somehow, these were God's words for *him*. This verse was *personal*.

Jumping from the page were words from Job 5:19:

"He shall deliver thee in six troubles: yea, in seven there shall be no evil touch thee."

Harry felt his pulse quicken and the hair stand up on the back of his neck.

In seven there shall be no evil touch thee.

40

He shut his Bible and closed his eyes. It was August, and the windows were open. A breeze wafted in with the smell of garden and fresh air and the sound of song birds. Harry felt energized and prayed, *God . . . I claim this as Your promise to me that I'll have my lung troubles for only six years. By then You'll cure me. I'm going to trust You for that. I feel that You still have some great work for me to do. If You still have plans for me, God, please confirm it to me somehow. But no matter what happens, Ill trust You, Lord. Amen.*

Not long after that, however, Harry's condition grew critical. Dr. Naught called in other physicians to confer regarding Harry's tuberculosis. They all concurred with the diagnosis as well as treatment. It was Dr. Naught who told Anna and Harry.

"Harry, you have to live *outdoors* in a more moderate climate, for the next *seven years*. Or else you won't live."

It was more than Anna could bear. First Luther, now Harry. She heard the physician's words as another death sentence. Anna broke down and began to cry and even Harry worked hard to control his own emotions. It was indeed a heavy statement.

"Why outdoors, doctor?" Harry asked.

"It's the latest treatment for the disease," he answered. "And Mrs. Crowell, you'll be interested to know that in nearly every case where this treatment has been prescribed, the patients have recovered their health. Some completely cured. There's a man, named Stetson, a hatmaker from Philadelphia. He had TB and went west for treatment. He joined the gold rush on Pike's Peak in '49 and was cured after seven years in the west."

"That's it!" Harry exclaimed.

His mother and the doctor looked at him quizzically. He told them that he'd found a passage in the Bible which he felt God was giving him as a confirmation that He still had work for Harry to do. "And I already knew it was going to be seven years. The Bible says, 'Seven years of troubles'."

"But how can he live outdoors? The weather is what is so hard on him now," Anna asked the physician.

"Oh, not in Cleveland. Somewhere that the climate's more sunny and warmer."

Over the next several days, the family discussed the situation and where Harry might go to rest and recuperate. Some friends of the family heard about it and dropped by to tell them about their recent return from Colorado.

They told Anna and Harry about Denver and the region just to the south. Summers there are cool, not humid. And winters are milder with lots of sunshine. Besides, they told the Crowells, it's a developing area, with lots of opportunities.

So, by September, Harry was ready to leave by train for Colorado.

Chapter Four

Harry Crowell stood on the train station platform restlessly as the porters carried his luggage onto the train. The smell of coal sulfur was thick in the air along with the sounds of hissing steam. The engine's bell and whistle all but drowned out normal conversation.

Uncle Joel gave Harry some last minute reminders about arrangements for getting money transferred once he was settled. His mother was more concerned that Harry would remember to take care of himself, and his fragile health. He reassured her over and over.

"I'll be fine, Mother. Dr. Naught says this will make all the difference in the world. I really must give it a try. Don't worry."

The train whistle gave a signal that it was time to go.

"All 'board!" the conductor shouted. "Better get yourself on the train, young man," he said to Harry.

"Good-bye, Mother . . . Uncle Joel." He bent to kiss his mother after which he shook hands with his uncle. Then he bounded up the steps and into the car. He waved from the window after taking his seat. In another few moments, the train began to move out and away from the station.

For several hours the train rattled smoothly over the flat plains of Ohio, westward into Indiana. Harry's thoughts raced madly. First, he was reminded of the times he'd taken a train eastward, to New England, to school at Greylock. *Greylock.* He wondered if President Mills had finished rebuilding the structure destroyed by fire and if his schoolmates were back in class in the new facilities.

Next, his thoughts turned to his father and he reflected at the wisdom Luther had shown by making provision for his family through careful estate planning. Without the money left for him by his father, Harry would have been unable to go to school and would never have been able to travel west to recover his health.

After awhile, he wondered what adventures were just ahead. What would he find out west? With these thoughts, Harry sat back in his seat and soon fell asleep. He napped for over an hour. He was awakened suddenly by a lurching of the train as it slowed to a stop in another station.

"South Bend," the conductor announced. It was late afternoon, and a number of passengers got off the train at this small stop in Indiana while others got on for the final leg of the trip to Chicago.

Harry took out his pocket watch and checked the time. "We should be in Chicago before it gets dark," commented the man in the seat across from him, as if reading Harry's mind. "Y'ever been to Chicago?" he asked.

"No, sir," Harry told him. "I've been East, but never this far west."

"You're in for a real time," the man told him. "I'm in sales. Get to Chicago a couple times a month. You won't believe your eyes. Y'know, even though I get back ever' couple a weeks, it's like a new city. In some places you'd never know they had a fire. Amazing."

Harry nodded. The Great Chicago Fire was legendary across the world. He knew about the devastation. He had seen the destruction of fire first hand last spring at Greylock when his school burned down, but the fiery loss of almost an entire city seemed hard to imagine. He listened as the salesman shared stories about the conflagration that had swept Chicago just three years earlier. Before long, the man looked up and out the window. "Well, you'll see for yourself soon. We'll be at the station before long."

The train began to slow as it finally pulled into the station yard. Harry was amazed to see dozens of tracks converging. Switch engines were shuttling freight and passenger cars back and forth in a chaotic choreography of noise and motion. Clouds of black coal smoke and steam created a haze that smelled of sulphur even with the coach windows closed. In a few minutes, the train was moving slowly into what seemed like a huge terminal. On both sides of the train were platforms, crowded with milling people, with more trains sitting on the adjoining tracks.

"Know where you'll be staying?" the salesman asked.

"What?" Harry was so caught up in the outside activity he didn't hear his travelling companion.

"This is the end of the line for this train. You're probably connecting here on another train, but I reckon it won't be leaving tonight. So, I was wondering where you're staying in Chicago."

"Uh, well, I'm not sure." Harry replied. "I suppose I'll just find a hotel nearby. Or maybe just wait in the terminal until my train leaves in the morning."

"Well, be careful of those downtown hotels. Their prices have gone up like a skyrocket since they rebuilt. By the way, my name's Elliot, Leroy Elliot." He shook Harry's hand. "I know of a couple smaller places that are reasonable. If you like, we can share a cab, check in and have a nice dinner. W'dya say?"

Harry nodded, retrieved his luggage and followed the portly salesman onto the platform toward the terminal. The immense size of the train terminal captured his eyes and thoughts. He tried to take it all in as he walked.

"This is the 'temporary' terminal. They built it when the other terminal was destroyed by fire. They're building a great new terminal over on Wells Street, but it won't be ready for a year or more. But even this temporary terminal is something, don't you think?"

As they walked through the terminal, he looked at the hundreds of travellers crowded onto the lobby floor, rushing either to trains or the curbside cabs.

Harry and Mr. Elliot finally managed to maneuver through the crowds to curbside. The street scene was every bit as frenetic as the inside of the terminal. One-horse cabs seemed everywhere, some parked, some weaving their way in and out of small clusters of other cabs. Peddlers shouted their wares, selling food, blankets, coffee and other drinks.

Elliot got a cab and piled their suitcases onto the seat. He climbed in, breathing heavily from the effort. He called out the name of a hotel to the cabbie as Harry climbed in and they were off.

The salesman described the "before and after" scenes as they passed. Harry imagined the devastation caused by the fire and was amazed at the reconstruction process. "Before the fire, everything was built of wood," Elliot explained. "It was a catastrophe waiting to happen. Now, they're using more sense."

As the carriage moved along the muddy, rutted streets, Harry took in the sights and smells. They were unlike anything he'd ever experienced.

"Tell you what, Crowell," Mr. Elliot said after a few moments. "Let's stop off here at Henrici's and get something to eat. I'll have the cab come back in an hour or so to take us to the hotel."

"Sounds fine to me," Harry said. "I'm famished."

The two men were seated at a table in a beautifully appointed dining room. As the waiter gave them each a menu and left them to consider their choices, Elliot pushed the menus aside. "We don't need 'em. This place is known for their great steaks. Tell you what, this'll be my treat. I guarantee you, you've never had a steak this good in your whole life."

"Well, that's most kind of you, but--"

"But nothin'. You're new in Chicago. And I crave someone to talk to over dinner. So I'll pay, and that's that!"

Harry smiled and shrugged. The waiter took their order for two steak dinners with all the trimmings, dessert and coffee.

The meal was everything Mr. Elliot boasted it would be. After dinner the waiter came by with a humidor of cigars. The salesman grabbed one and lit it but when he offered one to Harry he waved him off.

"Tell you what," Elliot said as he puffed clouds of blue smoke into the air, "I'll go pay the dinner bill and buy some more cigars. Then I'll see if the cab is back yet. You just stay here and relax 'til I get back."

Harry nodded. He watched as the salesman walked toward their waiter who was standing near the entrance to the dining room. Mr. Elliot said a few words to him, pointing to Harry, and the waiter nodded.

In a few minutes the waiter came over to the table. "More coffee, sir?"

"No, thanks," answered Harry. "I'm just waiting for my dinner companion."

The waiter looked quizzical. "But, sir, your companion has already left."

"Yes, he went to buy cigars and check on the cab."

"No, sir. I saw him get into a cab and leave. He told me just before he left that *you'd* be taking care of the check and I should put the cigars on the bill." The waiter handed the check to Harry.

Young Crowell felt the color drain from his face. The check was for what seemed to him to be a small fortune. Harry reluctantly reached into his wallet and peeled off several bills and paid the bill. Picking up his coat and luggage from the cloak room, he went outside to see if Elliot was still around, but he was sure he already knew the answer.

"Oh, there you are!" called a voice.

Harry turned and saw a small man standing beside a horse. "I'm here, just like your friend told me to be." It was the cab driver. "I got scared when you two didn't come. I thought you was pullin' a fast one and was gonna stiff me for the fare."

"B-But--" Harry stammered.

"You owe me for two fares from the train station to Henrici's, then for wherever you're goin' next."

"I'm afraid *I'm* the one who's been taken," Harry muttered. He paid the driver for the fare from the train station and explained how he'd just been *slickered*. "I'll just walk the rest of the way," he told the man.

The cabbie laughed. "Well, you been took, all right. But it coulda been worse. Some folks get taken for all they got when they come to the big city. You just had to pay for a lesson."

"I'll remember that," Harry grinned. It was true. Although he was angry at being so easily taken in, Harry was grateful that the salesman hadn't stolen all his money. The cab driver told him how to find an inexpensive hotel within walking distance and they parted company. Harry quickly found the hotel, checked into his room, unpacked and soon fell asleep.

*   *   *   *

The next morning, Harry was aboard a Union Pacific train leaving Chicago for the West. The big steam engine was pulling a long line of passenger cars, filled with people headed for Cheyenne and other points west.

All day long Harry gazed out the window, looking at new farmlands in Illinois, then Iowa. Night had fallen by the time the train reached Cedar Rapids and finally, at midnight, it rolled into Omaha, Nebraska. Harry fell asleep and dozed fitfully until daybreak, when again he looked out the window. The train was still in Nebraska, but now the flat, monotonous plains had evolved into hills and presented a scenic backdrop for the rising sun.

Before long, the train pulled into the village of Cheyenne, Wyoming. Harry was amazed to think that only a few years earlier, pioneers had trekked this same trail in covered wagons, taking many weeks--sometimes months--to cross the plains. It still represented the frontier of the American continent, but it was being tamed.

Just five years earlier, American plains and western lands were still at the edge of civilization. New settlers, along with the Army, battled Indians using rifles, cannon and six-guns against ancient weapons of bows and arrows. It was May 19, 1869, that the Union Pacific Railroad Line upon which Harry now rode, had completed the transcontinental railroad by linking up with the Central Pacific, which had started laying tracks from California.

It was difficult for Harry to imagine that only five years ago this was just a covered wagon trail. Now, he was part of an amazing achievement of transportation. Even before the West was tamed, the steam engine was making train travel routine. Telegraph lines ran parallel to the train tracks all along the way, tying the coasts with new communications in real time, as compared with mail sent by sea or by pony express.

This new travel and communications represented a quantum leap. Harry had been keeping himself apprised of these achievements, knowing that they'd soon *change everything* for business and society. Before, it often took decades for ideas to blossom and find their way into everyday life. Now, a thought in the mind of a Baltimore inventor could find its way (via the telegraph) into the head of a San Francisco engineer at the very same moment!

In like manner, trains could transport cattle, cotton, coal and other commodities in *days* instead of weeks or months. Foods could be fresh and more available. Cattle could be shipped by freight car alive to slaughterhouses in St. Louis and Chicago and the meat delivered right to the stores.

But as modernity overtook the eastern and central United States, in the west it was a different story. American Indians watched as if being invaded by aliens from a different world. The "iron horse", which rode on steel rails, brought farmers, miners, ranchers and speculators by tens of thousands, overwhelming both the land and various tribes.

At Cheyenne, Harry changed trains, boarding the Denver Pacific from Kansas City and heading now for the "mile high" city in Colorado. Denver had taken the nickname, "Queen City of the Plains" yet was little more than a lusty frontier town of 6,000 people. The train rattled along tracks laid snakelike along a trail east of the foothills of the Medicine Bow Mountains.

Harry watched the scenery change for most of the 101 mile trip to Denver. As the train passed south of Greeley, near LaSalle, he was suddenly jolted nearly out of his seat. The train lurched and shook. The shrieking sound of metallic brakes against the wheels frightened some of the passengers. As the train rattled to a stop, a nearby mother grabbed onto her seat and her tiny baby as her two-year-old tumbled to the floor. The toddler began crying loudly until her father picked her up.

The train was completely stopped now and there was noisy commotion as one of the conductors and two porters ran from the rear of Harry's car and down the aisle into the next car. Harry noticed that each of the porters were carrying large rifles and were grabbing at shells in a cartridge box one of them carried, trying to load the guns as they ran.

"What's going on?" Harry called out as they ran past.

"Don't worry, ladies and gents," the conductor yelled back. "Everything's fine. Just something blocking the tracks."

Harry went to his window and wrestled with the latch. The window opened and he stuck his head out to look. Ahead, where the engine stood idling with loud hissing of steam and noisy soundings of its whistle, Harry saw what appeared to be a huge river of blackness surrounding the engine and covering the rails. From this strange dark mass came animal-like sounds that Harry had never heard before. The sounds all but drowned out the noise of the train itself. Whatever it was had the ability to stop this huge train, showing no fear of the giant "iron horse".

Then Harry began to see individual animals inside the massive black form ahead. *Buffalo!* He'd heard of them, of course, and had read about them in school. He'd even seen drawings of them. But now, here in front of him, was a tremendous herd of *thousands*, perhaps even *tens of thousands*, of buffalo. A few strays ambled down the tracks toward him and his heart raced to see how massive they were. Standing taller than a man, and more massive than any other animal he'd ever seen, the buffalo grazed in the nearby prairie grass. They had long flowing brownish black coats and heads hung low with menacing horns.

Harry was absolutely transfixed by the sight. Up ahead, he heard the sound of gunfire. Now he understood the melee in the aisle minutes earlier. There would likely be buffalo steak or roast on the menu in the dining car tonight.

Despite the gunfire, train whistle and other noise, the buffalo were not easily run off. In a somewhat subdued stampede, the animals picked up speed as they crossed the railroad tracks on their way to greener pastures. Yet, even though they ran fast, it still took some ten minutes for the entire herd to cross in front of the train.

It was hard to imagine a herd of such immense size. Harry had heard tales of hunters from the east coming out to kill the animals. They skinned their kills and shipped the pelts back east to be made into robes, rugs and other decorations. In some cases, the animals were butchered for their meat, but most of the time, the carcasses were just left to rot in the sun since even by rail the dead animals could not reach the meat-packing plants before spoiling.

Still, travel clubs made up excursions to bring out hunters to shoot buffalo. There were so many animals it was never difficult for the hunting party to find them. Many times, the hunting parties didn't even have to leave the trains. They shot buffalo from windows and platforms of the cars, just for the "sport" of it, and didn't take either robes or meat.

Harry watched out the window. The two porters had shot several buffalo and were joined by several kitchen staff who quickly gutted and skinned the animals. Then they carved huge hunks of meat from the haunches and lugged them aboard the train. The carcasses were steaming in the autumn afternoon and it took several trips by five or six men to carry the meat onto the train.

Finally, the whistle sounded. Harry closed the window and watched as the herd melted into the distant dark hills. Settling back, he sighed as the train began to lumber forward. He was looking forward to arriving in Denver and checking into the Inter Ocean Hotel. When he wired for reservations earlier in the month, he learned that it was not just Denver's best hotel --it was the *only* hotel.

Chapter Five

The next morning Harry went downstairs to the dining room of the Inter Ocean Hotel. Perhaps it was purely psychological, but he already felt the benefits of the new climate. Except for getting used to the thinner air in the mountains, Harry found it otherwise easier to breathe. He had slept better last night, too.

As he entered the dining room, Harry paused to look around. The scene was so unlike anything he'd ever seen in Cleveland as to totally capture his attention. He stood for quite awhile just observing the people. A well dressed rancher sat at a table with two other men. All three were wearing the wide-brimmed Stetson style hats. The same was true at another table. Outside, sitting on the veranda, were several Indians in buckskin trousers and vests, but they also wore bright checkered flannel shirts, the kind worn by farmers or ranch hands. They sat patiently, as if awaiting instructions.

The taller Indian held a rifle in the crook of his arm and wore a belt of cartridges on his hips. Nearly every man Harry had met so far wore a pistol at his side and he felt a million miles from Cleveland, in another country altogether.

His gaze returned to the people in the dining room. He noticed a young man his own age sitting alone in the corner. There was a look of familiarity about him and as the man looked up, he saw Harry. His own eyes flashed with recognition and he called out.

"Harry! Harry Crowell!" The young man nearly knocked over his chair as he jumped up from the table and hurried over.

"George Worthington!" Harry exclaimed. "What are you doing here in Denver?"

George shook his head in disbelief. "I never in a hundred years expected to run into somebody else from Cleveland way out here."

"Neither did I," Harry smiled.

"My doctor sent me out here for my health. Says the mountain air will cure my consumption."

"That's amazing!" exclaimed Harry. "That's exactly why I'm here."

"Come on, sit down with me and have breakfast. We've got a lot to talk about."

George lived in Cleveland and although their paths had crossed once or twice, and they had mutual friends, the fact is they'd never gotten to know each other in Ohio. Now, however, it seemed a friendship quick in the making. For over an hour the two compared notes on things back home, how they'd both dropped out of school and how each had headed west in search of health.

"So, what are your plans?" George asked Harry at last.

"Well, I'm not so sure," Harry said. "This air seems easy enough to take--and I'm sure not anxious to act the invalid. What about you?"

"I've been here a couple weeks and I've already got cabin fever. I looked into a ranch not too far from here. I found out they'll give room and board in exchange for some chores. The doctor told me some moderate exercise would be all right, so I'll give it a try."

"That sounds like a good idea to me. Mind if I tag along when you go there?"

"You'll need a horse. Why don't we go across the street to the livery stable. I bought a nice-enough mare from them, and I think you'll find one to your liking."

*   *   *   *

Harry and George took to the outdoor life as if being born to it. At first, the two men were usually treated as *Eastern dudes* by the cowboys and regular hands on the ranches where they worked. It took a few weeks for blisters on their hands to turn into callouses, and a couple weeks longer for them to lose their saddle soreness and begin to feel comfortable riding horseback.

Because of their health, George and Harry adjusted more slowly to the strenuous life, but eventually they did and earned the respect of the experienced, grizzled cowboys. They took a nasty ribbing from the ranch hands on Saturday night, when the Ohioans chose not to go along into town for "lettin' off steam," as one of the hands put it.

Harry used his free time to read, usually from the Bible or some inspiring biography. George didn't read that much, but generally used his time to write home and re-read letters from his loved ones.

In the winter months, Harry and George impressed their cowboy friends by their skills on ice skates. None of the ranch hands had ever skated and those who tried it were as funny as circus clowns. They did not simply lose their balance and slip gracefully onto the ice. Rather, they fell with uncommon noise and bizarre movements, usually with arms flailing like opposing windmills, legs spreading widely and a wild, twisting at the hips. As they sprawled onto the ice, they would continue sliding--seat first--until they were stopped by some immovable object, like a tree or rock wall.

The Indians were both amused and amazed at George and Harry on ice skates. Nothing in their culture had quite prepared them for such a sight. But the two Ohioans were just as taken by the Indians using snowshoes to walk on top of huge drifts. They watched the Indians outdistance men on horseback trying to travel through snow drifts.

After nearly a year of living and working outdoors in Colorado, it was spring. When the flowers began to bloom and there was only a trace of snow on the mountain peaks, George and Harry decided to head back to Ohio for the summer.

Harry was pleased to see his family again, not fully realizing how homesick he'd been until he got back to Cleveland. The weeks in Ohio were pleasant and without incident. He had stopped in to see Dr. Naught, who seemed encouraged by the year in Colorado.

"But it's only a beginning," he told Harry. "You must spend seven years or more out West to find a cure."

"Six more years," Harry reminded the doctor. "I've claimed a promise in the Bible for healing after seven years. And I've already got one year behind me."

The doctor pursed his lips as if to speak, but he said nothing.

The people from his church were glad to see Harry, too. He chatted with them all, catching up on the news--which students in his class at Greylock went back to school and who was graduating, and who was going on to college in the fall.

One Sunday in church, Harry noticed a family he didn't recognize. Then he was more specific. "Who's that young woman?" he asked his mother.

"Why, you know her. That's the little Wick girl. Her family moved to Europe for awhile when she studied in Germany," Harry's mother explained.

"That's the little Lillie Wick? When I last saw Lillie, she was this high," he exclaimed, using his outstretched arm to indicate how tall she was when he last saw her, at age twelve.

Harry watched as she smiled and chatted with friends outside the church. Lillie was now a teenager, but seemed somehow older. She'd obviously been tutored in fine manners and graces. Harry listened to Lillie's musical laugh and gazed at her with a sense of warmth and appreciation.

"Yes, she really *is* beautiful," remarked Anna, seeming to read his mind.

As if this were the confirmation he was waiting for, Harry walked over to the Wick family and shook hands with her uncle, then her mother, finally with the lovely daughter.

"Hello, Lillie, it's good to see you again," Harry said softly as he introduced himself.   "Did I hear you've been away at school in Europe?"

Lillie smiled and chatted briefly with Harry, who resolved to see more of this young woman.

*   *   *   *

Lillie and Harry saw each other in church and in a few social settings over the summer, but he wondered about the age difference between them. He was twenty and she was five years younger. They became friends, but he did not court her in any serious way. By September she was off to school and he and George were back on the train west.

George and Harry spent a few hours in Chicago where Harry told his companion of his previous trip and how he'd ended up buying a con man dinner and a cab ride a year earlier. He and George were amazed at all the construction that had taken place during that year throughout Chicago. Newspapers trumpeted news of stunning inventions--a device that allowed two people in totally different places to carry on a conversation as if they were in the same room. It'd be a few years before the *telephone* exploded into common usage, but it was exciting to think about it.

And *typewriters*--machines that inscribed words onto paper, as if you had your own printer. And something called a *mimeograph* that made lots of copies of the typed documents. And there were stories about newly invented gasoline combustion engines that would replace steam engines, and make such engines more mobile.

Architects in Chicago had even found ways of stacking floors of office buildings on top one another creating *skyscrapers*.

Everywhere, inventions were becoming so pervasive as to have an effect on everyone's life. In 1875, half of the U.S. population still lived and worked on farms, but new mechanical inventions increased production and reduced harvest time and America began to ship more and more grain overseas.

"Harry, don't you sometimes think that things are happening too fast in the world?" George asked him as their train rolled westward. "I mean, everything is changing. All these inventions and new-fangled ideas might bring more problems than benefits."

"How do you mean?" Harry asked.

"Well, take the farmers, for instance. They've got steam combines and harvesters now, where one man can do the work of a whole threshing crew. And look at where we were in Colorado. How big would you say that spread was?"

"I'm not sure. Maybe five thousand acres," Harry answered.

"Back east, *nobody* could run a ranch that size. But in Colorado a crew of cowboys on horseback, with miles of that new *barbed wire* made into fences, can raise a thousand head of cattle. Don't you see, these inventions are gonna put people out of work. If you think the depression of '68 was bad, just think of what's ahead when machines take work away from people."

"I'm not sure that's the way it'll be, George. I mean, take ranching, just like you pointed out. The owners of these ranches are making so much more money they can hire more men to do different things."

"Don't you see," he continued. "These new things make more jobs possible because of the money and work they save. I don't think we have to be afraid of new things, George."

"Maybe so," his friend agreed. Then, the two settled back in their seats for the long trip to Cheyenne.

When the train finally arrived in Wyoming, the boys had agreed to try someplace else this year. Instead of heading to Colorado, they decided to go all the way to California. They sent telegrams back to Cleveland telling their families of their change in plans and took the train westward across the scrub desert and mountainous passes. Although it was still September, snow was already accumulating on the higher elevations.

After crossing the Sierras, the train began to go down the western slopes of the great mountains where eventually the landscape turned greener. Lush, tall ponderosa pines, oaks and trees that neither of them could identify cluttered the hills and horizon. They passed working mines not far from the tracks, saw farms and ranches, then soon were crossing the Sacramento Valley, with green grass and cattle. They were also surprised to see orchards and vineyards. The fragrance of oranges and lemons filled the air and was quite intoxicating.

Finally, the train came to the end of the continent--or so it seemed--at Vallejo, on the north end of San Francisco Bay. Harry and George were awestruck to watch as the train moved slowly onto what seemed to be a floating bridge. It turned out to be a train ferry that took the entire train across the water so it could continue to Oakland.

At Oakland, the passengers left the train for another ferry that took them to the opposite side of the Bay to San Francisco, a city of some 20,000 and growing daily.

Harry and George stayed in this bustling city and took in the sights, sounds and smells. It was a seaport and reminded Harry a little bit of Boston, but its buildings were new and more imposing--like those of Chicago rising from the ashes. San Francisco was also more cosmopolitan, with all races and nationalities. It was the first time George had ever seen an Asian, and Chinese seemed to be everywhere--with their long dress-like garb and small caps they energetically carried out all kinds of tasks.

Russian seafarers and fishermen were also in abundance. A Japanese ship was anchored at the wharf and its sailors were busily unloading cargo. As cargo nets were lowered by a series of ropes and pulleys, muscular longshoremen tugged at the other end of the ropes. These workers seemed composed of Irish or English laborers. Others were of European heritage. Some were black, probably sons of slaves freed a generation earlier.

Voices cried out instructions or sales pitches in English, Spanish and several other dialects that Harry did not recognize. It was amazing. The streets were filled with human variety and pandemonium. Horses and carriages tried to thread their way along narrow streets clogged with people. Here and there, some American Indians were seen. Most were wearing thick, colorful blankets over their shoulders and many had big, black Stetson hats with feathers stuck into the head band.

The city of San Francisco was filled with smoke from thousands of fireplaces, factory furnaces and cookstoves. It gave the air a pungency that both offended the senses and burned the eyes. The garbage and wastewater lying in the streets only added to the general pollution and led Harry and George to decide there was nothing in San Francisco to benefit them.

Before long, they boarded a tramp steamer that took them along the southern California coast to San Diego, by the Mexican border. San Diego itself was little more than a Mexican village of 2,000 people, but the two men decided to stay there.

For several weeks, they made the small town their base while they explored the surrounding areas. They bought a couple of horses and supplies and rode off to visit Escondido, El Cajon, Santee and Spring Valley--all within a 25 or 30 mile distance from San Diego. Then, Harry and George decided to head out further cross country. Leaving their base at San Diego with plenty of "grub" and other supplies, they rode back to Escondido, then went another 60 miles to Riverside.

From there, the two friends rode toward the San Bernadino Mountains. Although it was October, the weather was still hot and travel was dusty. They stopped at a few trading posts along the way, met a few miners and fortune-hunters and finally reached the Mojave Desert northwest of San Bernadino.

The Cereal Tycoon

Having spent a year in Colorado, neither of the men was not so inexperienced as to be called a "tenderfoot", but both were so unfamiliar with the desert and its dangers as to go on without difficulty. Rationing the water in their canteens, Harry and George rode their horses for the nearly fifty miles across the wasteland. They did have the good sense not to make the trip during the hottest part of the day and had started out before dawn when the air was still cold and the horses' watering trough had a thin layer of ice on it.

Halfway there, it got too hot to travel so they stopped to rest, waiting for late afternoon. Even so, by the time they were ready to ride again, the temperature was still 120 degrees.

Harry felt sorry for their horses, and held them to a walk despite their eagerness to cross the desert. He was grateful that they'd gotten used to California gradually with their day trips out of San Diego, and that when they'd gotten sunburned, they were close enough to San Diego as to not be terribly troubled by it. Now, although they were by now well tanned, the sun was unmerciful. Harry was grateful for their wide-brimmed Stetsons. He let the reins rest on the saddle horn as he wiped his neck and face with his kerchief.

"How much further?" George asked in a raspy voice.

"I'm not sure. From the map, I'd say another five, maybe six, hours."

"We should stop and make camp. We could start out before dawn, when it's cooler," George suggested.

"There's a full moon tonight. We can ride after sunset awhile. We need to get food and water for the horses. And our water won't hold out 'til much after sundown," Harry said.

About eight o'clock that night, the travellers finally made Palmdale where food, water and a place to unroll their blanket rolls awaited them. The next morning, refreshed and outfitted with supplies, the two men left Palmdale, heading north across still more desert to the town of Mojave, then northwest to Tehacapi Pass. It was cooler now that they were in the mountains, but the trade-off was that trail was steep and more difficult. Several times their horses lost their footing, but just as quickly they recovered.

As the days and weeks went by, the two men reached Bakersfield, Fresno, and finally, Merced. They had covered over 500 miles by horseback! Harry looked at their map and pointed out that Merced was almost directly east of San Francisco, where they'd started their journey after getting off the train in California. They decided to head back to San Francisco, but only after going to Yosemite. Winter was approaching, so the trail was often deep with snow. Many days, it melted, but as the days grew shorter, the snow stayed.

The two men were by now experienced trail riders so they decided to tour the entire valley of the Yosemite region, making sketches of the various peaks and camping out along the streams. The scenic wonders of their travels never became commonplace. Each day seemed to bring a greater sense of awe than the day before.

They decided to head west to San Francisco in time to make it by Harry's twenty-first birthday, January 27. Travelling in winter would slow them down, and the snow presented certain dangers--drifting, cold, avalanches--among them. It took longer than they'd planned to ride the 175 miles over the mountains, but they made it in time to celebrate in San Francisco on January 27.

The rest of the winter and spring, they took shorter adventures into the upper Sacramento River region. It was here the two of them fished the virgin streams for trout. With no worms to use for bait, the pair improvised, using a strip of red flannel on a hook. That's all they needed! The trout, and bass, too, fairly leaped onto the hooks.

They also hiked, climbed mountains, explored caves, studied wildlife, and wrote notes and letters about what they found. Amazingly, they explored an unusually large territory.

They were supposed to be recovering from illness, but even the more experienced outdoorsmen could not have done more.

Their accomplishments were all the more significant when adding into the equation their health, unfamiliarity with the land, the lack of maps, roads or hotels. The two eastern *city dudes* had taken on primitive California and mastered it, riding not too far behind the very first pioneers.

As summer approached, they talked about going home again.

"I want to see the 1876 Centennial Exposition in Philadelphia," Harry told his friend. "I can hardly believe that our country is already a hundred years old."

"Yeah," George agreed. "But I know the real reason you want to go back East. And her name isn't Philadelphia!"

Chapter Six

Harry was glad to see the Centennial Exposition that summer. It was a marvel of technological and industrial progress. He tasted of novel foods, some newly invented--like root beer--and others imported in refrigerated ships from overseas, like bananas. Virtually no one in the country had previously tasted such exotic fruit. Now, bananas would become commonplace. Harry also tasted canned ham, and fresh bakery goods made with European-imported yeast instead of the flat-tasting breads and rolls that everyone was used to.

Harry enjoyed the Exposition, but was even more pleased to return to Cleveland and resume his friendship with Lillie Wick. His absence for a year had proven the old adage about hearts growing fonder. It wasn't exactly a courtship, though, since George usually accompanied Harry to visit Lillie at her home on Spring Garden Street.

The three of them enjoyed the summer in Ohio, visiting fairs, going on picnics, telling Lillie of their visit to the Exposition and all the exciting things on display there. Before long, however, it was late summer and time to once more head west, so again the two men agreed to return to California.

Before he left Cleveland, Harry stopped for a physical examination by Dr. Naught. The physician was pleased with Harry's progress, but added, "You still have a long way to go."

"Yes, I know," replied Harry. "But you can't deny there's improvement. I'm counting on the promise of God that I found in the Bible--*'In seven troubles no evil shall touch thee.'* In a few more years, I'll be completely cured."

*   *   *   *

The fall and winter of 1876-77 were much like the previous year. Harry and George spent most of the time between Los Angeles and San Francisco, exploring the deserts and valleys. This time, though, they spent most of the winter months near the ocean, away from snowy mountain passes.

But by spring, they were ready for some serious mountain climbing. The year before, having explored and mapped the Yosemite Valley, about 175 miles east of San Francisco, they were eager to climb. They rode horseback into the valley which had only recently reopened--the roads and trails were impassable during winter. Yosemite had been discovered by white men just 25 years earlier. Farsighted state leaders made Yosemite a state park in 1864, deciding to preserve this natural beauty for its future citizens.

There were still several Yosemite Indian villages in the valley when the Ohioans passed through on horseback. *Yosemite*, Harry learned, meant *grizzly bear* in the Indian language. And there were plenty of these giant creatures still prowling, but they stayed mostly in the nearby forest. Yet, each of them carried a rifle in a saddle holster, just in case.

Harry and George had never seen anything like the gigantic sequoia trees growing in the Yosemite Valley. Loggers had proved a point by carving a huge arch out of the trunk of one tree. It was large enough to drive a covered wagon through! Harry surmised that a single tree could supply enough lumber to build an entire house--and maybe a barn to go with it.

Harry was spellbound by the scenic wonder of this place. There were spectacular waterfalls nearly everywhere you looked along the Merced River. Jutting above the valley floor were equally stunning granite peaks and rock domes. The names gave a clue to the seriousness with which the pioneers treated them: Hell's Mountain, Devil's Postpile and Devil's Gate, all within a day's ride.

The men decided to challenge Half Dome, rising to nearly 9,000 feet in the clouds. They stopped at a trading post and outfitted themselves with rope, heavy spikes and two small sledge hammers. The grizzled storekeeper sensed what their supplies were for, and told George, "This here ain't rope for climbin' mountains. It's *clothesline!* If'n ya wanna climb, you best get some heavier rope."

"But you said this is the strongest rope you've got," responded George.

"Yep, but it ain't meant for climbin'," the man said.

Harry and George were undeterred. They buckled on their canteens and some sandwiches in a backpack under the climbing tools, then set off. There was just enough slope for them to climb, stopping regularly to pound in spikes with the small sledges, onto which they tied off the rope. Slowly and perilously they attacked Half Dome.

The wind picked up and whipped at their faces. Despite their gloves and jackets, and the effort of pulling themselves up the mountain face, George and Harry felt pierced by the cold. They alternated positions as they climbed. First George would drive a spike into the granite rock, tie off the rope and hold it while Harry pulled up to where he was. Then Harry would take the lead. A few times, the spike came loose and almost pulled out when the rope was pulled on. At least once or twice the rope actually did come loose, but it happened at times the men were already on good footing.

Guardian angels must have been supervising their ascent and kept the ropes from breaking or pulling free of the support at critical times. Somehow, the inexperienced climbers reached the top.

On the summit, the wind was really severe. It whipped across the bleak rocks and slapped their faces. But Harry and George were oblivious. They seemed to be truly raptured. Looking across the Yosemite Valley, Harry could see the other peaks and domes of the region--El Capitan, nearly as high as where they stood; Mt. Lyell to the east; Mt. Hoffman, at nearly 11,000 feet, and finally, the spectacular Yosemite Falls.

After resting and having something to eat, they faced the prospect of returning to the ground below. George looked down from this dizzying height and recalled how long it had taken to climb up. At that rate, it'd be dark by the time they were only halfway down!

Harry seemed to know his friend's thoughts. "We'll have to find a different way to get down while it's still light. We sure can't stay up here all night. We'll freeze to death!"

"B-but, how?" George stammered. "The way we came up is the only way down."

Harry didn't answer right away. He was looking at the ropes, twisting them into a braid, stretching them out to determine their length. Finally he said, "I think if we put our rope together, like this, and tie off the sections, it'll reach that mound where the face really gets sheer. We can tie off the rope up here, then play it out as we go down. If we use it mostly for stability, and don't put our full weight on it, it should hold. Like this."

He demonstrated for George how he planned to go down. Harry took his sledge and tied the one end carefully around the steel hammer. Then he wedged it into a crevice in the rock where it wouldn't slip out. Then, looping the rope around his waist onto his left arm and wrapping several loops around his hand, he shook the rope. About twenty feet of slack were in the line between the crevice and the edge of the summit. Harry cautiously edged off the cliff and began to let himself down, stopping when the slack of the rope tightened, then feeding another section and repeating the process.

"It's all right if you don't look down!" he called back to George. When Harry was a quarter of the way down, his confidence grew. By now, he'd mastered the process and was able to leap ten or fifteen feet at a time, letting the rope stabilize his descent and planting his weight against the mountain as he fed out the rope.

George watched and fed off Harry's confidence. When at last Harry was safely at the base, George followed, slowly at first, then with greater agility. They left the rope where it was anchored, grateful for a safe and quick descent. Pumped with the adrenalin, the two men could hardly contain themselves as they packed up their gear and returned to the hotel where they'd already planned to stay the night.

In the dining room, over dinner, the men were still quite excited about their experience. At a nearby table, a couple of cowboys sat listening. One of them laughed out loud and called out to the Ohioans. "C'mon. Mountain climbin' ain't for pansies like you two. You two Eastern dudes are about as likely to climb ol' Half Dome as I am to play a parlor piano."

"Have *you guys* ever climbed Half Dome?" Harry challenged.

"Of course," the cowboy lied. "Lots of times. But I heard from Ed over at the tradin' post about your buyin' clothesline and all that. You two can put on quite a show, but you ain't gonna climb ol' Half Dome."

"Not again, probably," Harry replied. "But we already climbed to the summit earlier today. We came back down and got here just before supper."

"You can jaw all ya want, but you won't fool us," the other cowboy jeered. "Yer lyin'--there's jes' no way ya coulda done it."

George was about to get up and challenge the two men, but Harry put his hand on his arm. "Never mind, George," he said softly. "We don't have to prove anything. Wait 'til morning. They'll know."

It was true. The next morning the sun broke over the Cathedral Range and lit up the Yosemite Valley. George and Harry were saddling their horses in front of the hotel when the two cowboys came out. All ready to resume their taunting of the two Easterners, they looked over at Half Dome where the sun was reflecting off its face.

"W-well, I'll be--" the first cowboy stuttered.

"I c'ain't believe it!" the other man called out.

Fluttering in the wind was the rope Harry and George had used to scale Half Dome and descend. From this distance, it looked more like a spiderweb than a clothesline. And when the two cowboys did a closer inspection later that morning, they found the spikes hammered into the granite which the two *dudes* had used to pull themselves skyward.

For the rest of their time in Yosemite, their reputation was made. Word travelled about the two men from Ohio who climbed the dangerous and difficult peaks and domes within the valley, and new respect was accorded to them.

Several weeks later, the two young men separated. George decided to stay in California, but Harry made up his mind to go back East. His affection for Lillie made him especially want to spend time in Cleveland, but first, he planned to go to Philadelphia.

Dr. Weir Mitchell was a specialist in illnesses like his and Harry wanted him to do a thorough examination and determine his exact physical condition. Harry had noticed real improvement following his three years in the West, but was anxious to have an expert opinion.

It was an exhilarating time. The physician told Harry that there was indeed real progress being made. But he cautioned, "Remember, you must keep up this regimen for another three years."

Harry left the doctor's office with his head spinning. Maybe he could make plans after all; perhaps he would be cured. He lifted a prayer of gratitude to God for keeping His word.

*   *   *   *

Harry's enthusiasm led him to want to share his good news. He had told Lillie soon after their first time together about the reasons for his trips out West, and his search for a cure for his tuberculosis. She understood and had encouraged him with her letters and prayers. Now, as Harry returned to Cleveland, he was eager to share Dr. Weir's good report.

There seems to be no good reason, Harry thought, *that we should not be engaged now.*

Lillie, now seventeen, was a lovely young woman. He did not bring up the subject of his real mission at first, but just let the conversation evolve naturally. Then he told her of his visit to Dr. Mitchell and the good report.

By the time their reunion ended, he got the courage to bring up the subject of an engagement. It was then that he learned that Lillie had also been thinking about it. So, after many hours of summer conversations and courtship, he proposed. By the time he was to return West in the fall, they were engaged.

Harry returned to California where he met George Worthington for their final year together. George had nearly regained full health, and as they toured California through the spring of 1878, he had recovered enough to go back and take his place in business. This left Harry to think about making long range plans for himself.

Now he had the incentive to plan ahead. His health was improving, he was engaged to be married. But what business should he take up?

He thought about the question often during that final year in the West with George. One day, he met a man who told him about the attractions of North Dakota. A town had been laid out by Bill Fargo of the Northern Pacific Railroad which already had a population of 800. The man described the area as "an empire in the making."

"The plains go on forever," he told Harry. "It's perfect for farms and cattle ranches. Everyone who gets in is going to get rich," he promised.

Harry thought about that but wanted to do some checking on his own. There was always someone promising a "get rich quick" scheme, but few plans held up after careful scrutiny and research. Yet, this time, the man seemed to know what he was talking about. Harry decided to visit Fargo and check on the land. It would have been practical to stop on the way back from California and spend the time necessary to check out the area.

Instead, Harry felt he must hurry back to Cleveland. He usually returned in early summer, but this time he was compelled to come back in early spring. The reason was in Lillie's most recent letters to him. She had written:

Dearest Harry,

Our engagement has given my mother great sorrow. She insists that I break off with you. I do not know what to do, as I cannot bear to hurt her. Since Father died, she is so lonely. She fears that your fate is the same as that of my Father; that you will not live to raise a family and care for your wife. She does not want for me to be left a widow as

*she was. I do not know what to tell her. I wish you were
here to advise me.*

Harry wrote back at once, trying to convince Mrs. Wick
that he would regain his health, and that she should not worry.
But she would have none of it. Harry told her of the good
reports from Dr. Mitchell in Philadelphia and his own
assurances from the Scripture that he would be cured. However,
Mrs. Wick was adamant. She insisted that Lillie break the
engagement for she could never give them her blessing. Lillie,
caught in the middle, felt helpless.

In her letters Lillie told Harry how she'd cried herself to
sleep nearly every evening he was in California, so torn was she
by this issue.

He came back to Cleveland, anxious to convince her
mother by his presence and progress. "You can see how I am
recovering my health," he pleaded. "In the West, I am able to do
everything other able-bodied men can do. You must believe me
when I tell you that I will soon be fully cured."

"I'm sorry, Harry," Mrs. Wick told him emphatically. "I
cannot, I will not, have my daughter become a widow. It is
impossible! How either of you could even contemplate such a
disaster is beyond me!"

Lillie began crying, then her mother also broke down.
Soon the two women were holding each other, sobbing together.
Now it was Harry's turn to feel utterly helpless. He decided to
leave, hoping that in the light of another day, logic would
prevail. The next day, however, Lillie sent a note to Harry
telling of her decision:

Dearest Harry,

*Please know that my love for you is great, but my duty is
clear. I must act in accordance with the wishes of my dear
mother and thereby ease her grief and despair. I accept the
full responsibility for not thinking how she has been
troubled deeply by Father's death, and does not wish her
daughter to have a similar calamity befall her. With a*

*crushed heart and out of concern for the grief of my mother,
I must regretfully break our engagement.*

*　　　*　　　*　　　*

On April 29, 1878, Harry left Cleveland for Fargo, wondering if his dreams and plans were unraveling. As the train rattled northward, he tried to ease his grief by reading, to no avail. Then he watched the landscapes flying by out the window. Nothing cheered him. The train crossed Wisconsin, then Minnesota. Just five miles over the Minnesota state line was Fargo, his destination.

Harry took a room at a downtown hotel, got a horse from the local livery, and spent several weeks just roaming the area. He rode along the Red River and the Sheyenne River, fished in nearby Minnesota lakes and watched summer come to the northern plains.

Half-heartedly he checked the claims of the man he'd met in California. It seemed true enough: there were vast grazing lands and some were already starting to raise cattle and horses. Money could be made, for sure.

The more he became engrossed with prospective business, the less he was troubled by his broken engagement. Finally, after praying for guidance, he decided to act on the business proposition. He set up an appointment with a local real estate developer.

The real estate agent told Harry about two sections of land for sale--1,280 acres--a parcel that had once been part of Indian lands and had never been farmed before.

"How much?" Harry asked him.

The man gave Harry a figure and the Ohioan shook his head, telling the agent to offer a much lower price.

The real estate man came back a bit later. "Do you still want to buy?"

Harry nodded. "At my price?"

This time the real estate man nodded. "Then the deal is closed."

Harry rode out to see the land, some twelve miles south of Fargo. He traded his saddle horse for a horse and buggy to make the long commute. The several hours it took to drive to the farm gave Harry time to read, draw plans, figure the numbers and think about his projects along the way, making better use of the time.

By May, 1878, he had built and stocked the farm. A big barn was erected, housing the mules and horses. One entire section was plowed and planted with wheat. Harry had learned to be alert to new ways of doing things, to not be so dependent upon traditional methods. The American West, and its plains, were different than anything farmers had seen before. In Minnesota, Iowa and Nebraska, the topsoil ran as deep as several feet (instead of the usual several inches found elsewhere) and it was virgin soil--rich with nutrients. The wild grasses sometimes grew as tall as a man, and cattle--like the buffalo-- could survive, even thrive, on these grasses despite the severe winters on the plains.

When the wheat had ripened and reapers had cut and stacked the grain in the field to dry, Harry started his usual drive back to Fargo from the farm one evening. He hadn't gone far when he noticed a black funnel cloud rushing toward his farm.

Harry had heard about these storms, and had even seen a tornado devastate a nearby town in his native Ohio when he was a boy. He knew it could be fatal if a person was caught in its path, so Harry hurried his horse and buggy toward Fargo to escape it, keeping his eye on the quickly approaching tornado.

Even here, so far away from the dark and terrible funnel, the storm was intense. Lightning exploded in nearby tree-tops and thunder spooked his horse so much that Harry used all his strength just to keep control of the reins.

The rain began to pelt him, along with hail. But he was still several miles from Fargo, and sanctuary from the raging winds. Looking over his shoulder, Harry watched the funnel cloud, dark and moving steadily and inevitably to the East. He knew that his farm and crops were going to be hit, destroying everything Harry had built. Instead of making money, now he was certain to lose everything he'd invested, except perhaps the price of the land itself. He prayed urgently for God's help.

Finally he reached Fargo, and the safety of the livery stable and hotel. The tornado avoided Fargo, keeping to its easterly track, as far as Harry could tell. The darkness of the storm blended into nighttime, and a calm settled over the town.

Harry hardly slept that night. He tossed and turned in his bed, praying and sleeping restlessly. Early the next morning he drove his horse and buggy back to what would be left of his farm. Along the way, he was stunned at the terrible damage. He was glad to have left when he did and hoped all of the farm hands had taken to the cyclone cellars early enough to have safely sat out the storm.

Those who hadn't taken shelter would certainly not have survived, Harry thought. Trees were uprooted and tossed about. Fields of wheat were flattened and destroyed. Here and there, farmhouses and barns were unrecognizable as such. The farmhouse next to his, a beautiful new place like his own, was gone. Clothes that were hung on the line the day before had beem strewn by winds into the tops of trees for miles around. The neighbor's stacks of grain were likewise scattered, some tossed five miles away, across the river.

The closer Harry got to his farm, the worse the destruction. As he approached the lane to enter the property, his eyes widened. There was absolute devastation on both sides, but his big barn was still standing, untouched! So was the farmhouse. The livestock was unhurt. Even the shocks of grain in the fields still stood where the farmhands had stacked them after harvest. And the hands themselves were going about their chores, all safely delivered from the storm.

He couldn't believe it! Harry got out of the buggy and surveyed for damage. When he checked, he discovered that the tornado had taken a straight line course directly at his farm, not veering at all for two miles. Then, miraculously, at the last minute, the storm had suddenly turned left, sparing all of his crops and buildings.

Harry told the story of his good fortune to everyone in Fargo who would listen. That evening he repeated it over dinner at the hotel. "It was a miracle," he told his listeners. "God changed the direction of that tornado and spared my farm."

"Then maybe you want to sell your farm?" someone asked. Harry turned to another table and recognized the real estate agent who sold him the land.

"Sell? I just bought it and built the farm. Why would I sell now?"

"Profit," the real estate man replied.

"Profit? What do you mean?" Harry asked him.

"I've got a man from Erie, Pennsylvania--just came into town and wants to buy a farm just like yours. Will you sell?"

Harry thought for a moment. His reasoning was simple: *Lord, You saved my farm and crops. Now it appears You've sent someone offering to buy the property. Do You want me to sell?* He began figuring his costs and added on good profit, then named that price.

The real estate man nodded. "That's within the range he gave me to work from."

"Cash. No contract sale," reminded Harry.

The man held out his hand. They shook and the deal was done.

"What other property do you have?" Harry asked the real estate man.

"Well, let me see." He took off his hat and thought for a moment. "I have a most exceptional tract of land down in

South Dakota, a few miles east of the Sisseton Indian Reservation, near the Red River. It's south of Wahpeton, about seventeen thousand acres all told."

Many would have choked on the size of such a parcel but after agreeing on price Harry took an option on the land. The purchase price, however, was much more than the money he had cleared after selling his farm. So Harry decided to return to Cleveland and get advice from his uncle, William Waite.

Uncle William was impressed with his nephew's first business venture. "Not too bad for such a 'sick' man," he teased, alluding to the reason for Harry's broken engagement.

The next day, his uncle introduced him to his own Cleveland banker and asked Harry to recount his story. The banker smiled as he heard of the young man's success.

"And now you want to buy another tract of land?" the banker asked Harry.

"Yes, sir."

"How big?"

"Seventeen thousand acres," Harry answered.

The banker sat back in his chair, startled. "Did you say seventeen *thousand?*"

Harry nodded.

For a moment no one spoke. Then the banker looked over at Uncle William. "Well, if you think he can do it, so do I. We'll approve the loan."

On the way back from the bank, his uncle asked how Harry planned to make this project work.

"Well, I'm not sure," he admitted. "It's really much more than I can imagine as a wheat farm. Seems to me I'd be all summer just plowing to put in seeds."

His uncle agreed. "Horses. That's what I'd do."

"Really?"

Harry listened as Uncle William talked about his own hobby, raising Percheron draft horses. "Don't you see, every farmer in your area will need these big draft horses in order to farm such big tracts of land. And they'll pay good prices for them. Why don't you go on ahead, close on the land, and get set up. It'll give you time to build the barns, house, and other buildings. By then it'll be winter. You can come back here in the spring and I'll travel all through Ohio with you to find enough Percherons to start a breeding herd."

That's exactly what Harry did. By spring, 1879, the two men had scoured central Ohio to find the stock, buying up some 300 healthy mares and a majestic stallion then brought them back to Cleveland. Harry contracted with the railroad to make up a special train, just for shipping the several hundred Percherons to South Dakota.

It was an event to be talked about for the next fifty years. Harry had giant billboard size signs painted on the sides of the box cars carrying the horses. The colorful cars had big banners proclaiming the *Red River Percheron Parade*, as the train was called, and it brought people out to stare all along the Northern Pacific route. The horses were taken off the train at Fargo and herded to the new ranch in South Dakota, almost fifty miles south.

The event was a marvelous marketing idea. By now, word had reached farmers for many miles around. All had heard of the great *Red River Percheron Parade*. Many had never seen such huge draft horses before. These creatures had nearly twice the muscular bulk of an ordinary saddle horse, and the sound of their huge hoofs on the dry ground could be heard at quite a distance.

The farmers were genuinely impressed and could immediately envision how the horses could be put to use behind a plow or heavy grain wagon right on their own farms. Harry was creating a market for the Percherons even before they were ready to sell. The Percherons were the main topic of conversation wherever the farmers congregated, and each man explained how he'd best use such horses.

In fact, the Crowell Farm was soon the talk of three states even as the young entrepreneur set about making his dreams become reality. He had already attracted much attention when he began the project a year earlier.

To house so many draft horses, a number of barns and other buildings had to be built. Harry had hired crews, ordered materials, negotiated deals, helped assemble machinery and trained his help with instructions from Uncle William on the care and raising of Percherons. All this preparation had taken place before the horses were even selected and brought to the farm, and that by itself was enough to fuel local conversations. But now, the train had brought the horses, and the project was clearly visible, and the talk was at its zenith now.

*   *   *   *

Without her mother knowing, Lillie had continued to write to Harry, a bittersweet situation. He treasured her letters but was often stung by the words, as in the case when she spilled her despair:

> *Dear Harry,*
> *It seems as though you and I are to travel a thorny path to*
> *heaven. . . . If such is the Lord's will, I will submit.*
> *Affectionately, Lillie*

Then, when Harry came home to Ohio to purchase the horses with his uncle, both Lillie and her mother saw him. He seemed to be a totally different person than the young man with dubious health they had met the year before.

Lillie told a friend, "When Mother and I saw Harry's improved condition, my hope was revived."

Then, mustering up the courage to do so, Lillie got the name and address of Harry's specialist in Philadelphia and sent him a letter:

Dear Dr. Mitchell,
When we were engaged, Mr. Crowell being then so delicate,
Mama feared his recovery to perfect health impossible, and
the idea of her dying and leaving her fatherless and only
child with an invalid husband drove her to despair.
Knowing the trouble she has passed through, and with the
desire to lighten this last burden, I sacrificed the fondest hope
of my life and broke the engagement. . . . but Mr. Crowell
returned to Cleveland, April 21, with so decided an
improvement in every respect that both Mama and I are
greatly encouraged. . . hope revived! . . . . Do you think Mr.
Crowell's health will ever permit our hope to be realized?
                                    Lillie Augusta Wick

                    *   *   *

Dr. Mitchell wrote her back:

My dear young lady,
A girl so true and devoted as you, and who can make such
a sacrifice, deserves that a doctor should come in like the
third volume of a novel and make the paths straight.   Let
me advise you.   Tell Mr. Crowell I think he will get well at
the cost of two or three years on a farm . . . tell him I must
see him then . . . then it will be time enough to talk of a
renewed engagement.

Harry and Lillie did not discuss a renewed engagement.
Their letters were friendly, newsy and inspired each of them to
not throw away their feelings for the other.

Meanwhile, Harry found and hired a good foreman for
the farm. The work began to thrive. They put the draft horses
to work immediately and planted twenty-five hundred acres of
the huge farm in wheat, expecting 25 bushels of grain to the acre
at harvest.

Then, a dry spell struck just as the grain heads were forming. Hot, dry winds--and no rain--shrivelled the wheat. Instead of 25 bushels to an acre, Harry harvested eleven.

It was frustrating and discouraging for Harry. For the first time, he had no control over the elements that created success. In normal business, he could step in and correct things when they went wrong. But in farming, he could not do anything about tornadoes or drought. He wondered, *Did I make a mistake? Should I give up farming? If so, what'll I do then?*

As he had with his other venture, Harry prayed for guidance. And as before, God answered miraculously, almost immediately. A businessman from Minneapolis had heard about the Percherons and instinctively suspected what Harry and his uncle had concluded about the success of their plan.

"The fact is," the businessman admitted, "You've already 'sold' the farmers on these horses. That train stunt was magnificent. Great advertising. Now everyone within 300 miles wants one of your draft horses."

As the man talked, it was apparent he wanted to buy everything--land, horses, buildings, livestock--all of it. Harry listened, but didn't reveal his own interest in wanting to sell.

The man persevered and the two finally discussed price and terms. Then, a deal was struck and the whole enterprise was sold. He wrote his uncle to tell of the success:

Dear Uncle William,

I've sold everything at a good price. I am confident: God was guiding. I also feel that I am in good health again, and I have completed my seven years in the out-of-doors. After selling the farm I've reasoned that God does not ask me to stay out-of-doors any longer. So I'll return to Cleveland and see what He will show me next.

Your nephew, Harry Crowell

Chapter Seven

The fall of 1880 should have been a time of celebration and happiness, but Harry Crowell felt something missing in his life. True, his health had been regained--the doctor pronounced him cured of his tuberculosis. And his first major business ventures were highly successful. Yet, he was still stung over his broken engagement with Lillie Wick.

But as he thought about it, Harry decided to simply wait out the situation. He had, after all, patiently endured the seven years of imposed rest in order to regain his health. What was another few months, or even a year, of waiting for Lillie's mother to change her mind about him.

Patience is indeed a virtue, he thought. He wondered what might have happened if his father had not given in to the inevitability of the disease that had killed him. True, Luther Crowell had faced up to death, and prepared for it. *But what might have happened if the doctor had prescribed for Father what he laid out for me?* Harry asked himself. *Was there anything that Father could have done to fight it? Did he give up too quickly?*

Harry determined that he would not give up. He saw this quality as one which would help him eventually win Lillie, but more than that, it would be a quality that would set him apart from others in future decisions about business and life:

Do not be in a hurry. Give the matter time. Do not give up too quickly.

*   *   *   *

Another year passed with Harry staying in Cleveland. He had been able to visit Lillie often, and her mother's fears were slowly eroded. Both women could see a man of robust health, and Mrs. Wick's arguments lost their effectiveness.

80

In November, Lillie turned 21. And the occasion proved doubly satisfying because Harry's patient and undemanding manner had won them over. At last, Lillie and Harry were engaged to be married. The couple set the date for a spring wedding.

Interestingly, it was this same year that the tuberculosis bacillus was discovered. Now those with the disease could be cured more easily with a vaccination rather than the stringent regimen of living outdoors that Harry had just completed.

But Harry did not dwell on the irony of that. He was now engaged; he had to make plans for suitable business ventures to provide for a wife and family. Once again he was reminded of his covenant with God made the night he heard D. L. Moody: *God, if You will allow me to make money, I will keep my name out of it, so You will have the glory.*

As he reflected over his first two ventures, it seemed obvious to him that God had kept His part of the bargain. As a boy, young Crowell had learned early lessons in faith from his pastor, Dr. Hawks, and his faith had matured during the seven years in the "wilderness" where he learned physical, mental and spiritual lessons. He was now ready, having a strange assurance that his works were in God's hands--that with his own stewardship, the plans would mature into great wealth or other success. So, Harry felt compelled to bathe his next venture, whatever it might turn out to be, in prayer and soul searching.

It was his uncle, Joel Parsons, who approached him with an idea. A wholesale grocer in Cleveland, Uncle Joel had bought a mill in a nearby town and offered it to Harry. "Timing is everything," Joel said to his nephew. "I think this venture brings together several central ideas and situations where the value of each of them independently doesn't begin to approach the value of all of them combined."

"What do you mean?" Harry asked.

"Well, I'm not sure I can explain it. You'll have to look into it yourself," he replied.

His uncle then told him about the small grain mill in nearby Ravenna, Ohio. At first, Harry could see nothing notable about this old stone mill in the center of a quiet, rustic village. It seemed to him like every other mill he'd ever seen. His interest was not at all piqued, even when he began to research the venture.

The Quaker Mill, as it was called, was in financial trouble when Uncle Joel acquired it. Its present owner, Warren Corning, bought it from two men who started the business but had lost money in it. Corning ran it for two years, but also ran into serious reversals, and wanted to sell, which is how Joel Parsons had come by it.

Now that his uncle had offered it to him, Harry looked into the situation and learned quite a bit from other owners of mills. As they explained, the business was quite straightforward. Not much had changed in the art of milling, even after thousands of years. Harry recalled that even in the Bible, there were stories telling about women making flour by using two stones to grind the grain. This method of grinding, the *quern* method, was mostly unchanged since the time of Christ.

Over the centuries, only the form of power changed, first driven by slaves, animals, and eventually by water and steam. Yet the method stayed essentially the same. Harry decided that the milling business, even with industrial applications, was still at least a century behind the times. However, the Ravenna Quaker Mill employed a revolutionary new method, involving rollers and cutting blades invented by one of its founders.

The mill also specialized in milling oats. Until now, most Americans thought of oats as horse food, not something for humans--unless they were Scottish immigrants with a taste for oatmeal porridge.

As part of his homework in evaluating the Quaker Mill, Harry inquired of others as to the value of oat milling. In fact, that's how he had heard of Ferdinand Schumacher, a German pioneer who emigrated to America early in the century. Schumacher started out as a salesman, selling notions, then groceries. It was in the grocery store that he remembered selling something in his native Hamburg, Germany--cracked oats. So he rigged up a device for cutting oats into miniature cubes and sold them over the counter in his store.

The cracked oats had to be cooked for hours before they could be eaten, but the nourishment from such a simple meal helped to sell his new product. He bought a mill to expand production of cracked oats but ran into problems in finding efficient ways to cut the hard kernels of oats.

In 1875, one of his employees, William Heston, invented a device for cutting oats which was efficient in ways never before seen. Heston rushed out and patented his invention and assigned it to Schumacher, but with some strings attached. The conditions included that Schumacher would have the rights to the patent, but that Heston would also have the right to use the invention in any mill in which he (Heston) was interested.

Since Heston had been one of the organizers of the Quaker Mill, the patent rested there as one of the assets. Another intangible asset was the Quaker name. Harry immediately saw its value in what it conveyed to the public: strength, integrity, trust, quality.

Harry sat in his study going over his notes on the Quaker Mill. He had visited the site several times and was familiar with its buildings and grounds. For some reason, he had expected that Quaker Mill would be a small, quaint stone building with a big water wheel on the banks of a small river, similar to those in every New England and Midwestern town of the 19th century. This one, however, was different. It had been built only a few years earlier and consisted of several new buildings and grain bins. The mill itself was run by steam engines in the three story building adjacent to the equally tall grain storage bins.

Now he understood what his uncle meant by the combined value of its assets having more worth then each of them independently. And timing. An industrial age had been launched and the lifestyles of entire cultures were being changed. In America, fewer than half of its population still remained on farms. The rest of them had moved into the cities to find work in factories. As such, most people had neither the time nor resources to enjoy the huge breakfasts they had grown up with on the farms. Nor did they have to face the intense physical labor they'd had on the farms.

Harry could foresee the breakfast habits of an entire nation changing, and he also envisioned how a nutritious breakfast of Quaker oats could make the mill profitable. Young Crowell learned that oats appeared rather recently in history. They are not mentioned in the Old Testament story of Joseph, where grain was stored in Egypt. Some think oats originated in South America, off the coast of Chile. And exactly when oats appeared in America is uncertain. They are mentioned as being planted in Colonial days and became an important cash crop by the 1800s. But most people still thought of oats as horse food.

Harry, now 26 years old, approached the business with youthful enthusiasm and ideas. He had no time for those who thought he was too young and his ideas too untried. His was a revolutionary vision, with bold ideas on how to make the business work.

With the new rolling cutters, the oats could be milled and packaged for mass market consumption. Recent studies in vitamins and nutrition showed that the product was rich in vitamin B-1, calcium, and riboflavin. Oats were also rich in iron and protein as well as other good elements for "building bodies". The product had value and its methods of manufacturing were likewise sound. What was needed was a method for creating a market for and then merchandising the oats to that market.

Harry finally made up his mind to buy the Quaker Mill from his uncle. Then he invited Jim Andrews to manage the business for him. Jim was a relative of sorts. He was the younger brother-in-law of his uncle, Joel Parsons, (brother to Joel's wife and Harry's aunt, Amelia).

The men began immediately to make the business work. During the week, Harry and Jim Andrews labored in Ravenna, some 35 miles from Cleveland. Jim was proving to be the best part of the acquisition; he was a dependable and tireless worker. He was able to know intuitively when things were wrong with the equipment, or when machinery might fail. He anticipated problems and made the mill run smoothly while Harry worked on the problems of merchandising and marketing.

On weekends, Harry drove back to Cleveland to spend time with Lillie. The two of them were married on June 29, 1882. Lillie's mother was unable to attend. She was ill in Philadelphia and under the treatment of doctors there.

Harry and Lillie moved to Ravenna right after their marriage, but moved back to Cleveland nearly a year later, after Lillie learned that she was expecting a child.

On May 3, 1883, a daughter, Annie, was born. Annie was named after Lillie's mother, who was the baby's godmother. Following her birth, the Crowells took up residence in the Stillman Hotel in Cleveland. The grand, eight story hotel apartment was near the home of Lillie's aunt who often came to visit. The place also became Harry's refuge from the daily business problems. These were difficult times of deep economic trouble in America. Competition was fierce, and many businesses failed. All in all, these were dark times that tested their faith.

*   *   *   *

The most difficult testing of Harry Crowell's faith came nearly two years later, just after Christmas, in January, 1885. Lillie had not been feeling well for some time, apparently sick with a flu. She told Harry not to worry, that her aunt would stop by and help take care of Annie, now 19 months old. The snow was especially deep on the roads to Ravenna and it was difficult for Harry to make the trip back and forth to Cleveland more frequently, so he decided when Lillie didn't improve to stay at home with her.

The doctor came to the Stillman Hotel and gave Lillie medicine and urged rest, but she seemed to be growing worse, and Harry was frightened. He stayed awake nights with her, praying for her, holding her hand and lovingly wiping her brow. He didn't go to the mill or leave or side. With the lack of sleep and concern for his wife, his own health began to suffer. Fatigued and aching from sitting up nights in a chair beside her bed, Harry hung on and prayed. But then, on January 10th, Lillie suddenly died.

Her husband was grief-stricken and inconsolable. For weeks afterward Harry felt as if his world had collapsed. Lillie's mother, Mrs. Wick, had recovered her health, and had earlier returned to Cleveland. Now she was a source of strength to Harry, carrying for the baby, fixing meals and helping out in other ways.

"It's terribly ironic," she confessed to Harry one day. "My fears were that you would die and leave her a widow. Now, for her to die . . . and so young--" She didn't finish the thought, but Harry knew what was on her heart.

Harry told her his own thoughts. "For all those years I was away, I made plans for us. I dreamed of our life together. I assumed that it would be forever. My father died long before my mother. I naturally figured Lillie would outlive me by many years." Then he added sadly, "I--I seem to be utterly lost without her."

"Yes. I know," Mrs. Wick said sympathetically. After a long pause in the conversation, she asked him, "Harry, what about the baby? Have you thought about her?"

"What do you mean?" he asked.

"She needs a mother. She's at a critical time in a child's life. She needs constant attention and nurture. How will you provide for her needs?"

Harry had been thinking about Annie also. Lillie's aunt had been recruited to help just after the death of the young 26-year-old mother. But she was unable to give on-going care for the baby.

"I've been thinking, Harry," Mrs. Wick said. "The doctors told me that my health is improved enough that I could help."

The young husband and father hadn't considered that Annie's grandmother might be the one to care for her. Then he recalled that Mrs. Wick was the child's godmother as well as grandmother. She had given the couple her commitment to care for their daughter if something had happened to either of them. That had been her promise at Annie's birth.

"Harry, let me take Annie. I'll raise her as I did my own child."

After much prayerful thought and consideration, Harry agreed. Annie went to live with her grandmother.

Following the terrible death of his young wife, Harry plunged himself fully into the business of the Quaker Mill. Eventually, his pain subsided, or at least dulled somewhat, but there were still many times that memories of Lillie and their times together would release the pain and tears.

Harry ached for her, and it seemed as if every event, every situation, still held fond and precious memories. Many of these recollections made his heart skip and cause a catch in his throat when he thought of Lillie.

Chapter Eight

Harry Crowell busied himself with the routine administration of the Quaker Mill business while Jim Andrews took care of the production. They both worked hard, but the fledgling business seemed to have a difficult time moving ahead.

As he'd done with other ventures, Harry made the business a part of his daily prayers. He asked for God's wisdom in how to increase production; how to merchandise; how to sell the products. Devout friends and even some family members weren't used to giving over such matters for divine guidance. Yet, to Harry, all of life was stewardship and worthy of God's interest and direction.

As he thought about merchandising the rolled oats, Harry came up with the idea of packaging them in clean, attractive and colorful boxes for individual sales. Before that, oatmeal was sold from barrels or boxes set on the floor in grocery or general stores. As a result, the oatmeal was usually contaminated with insects, worms and vermin. The customers had no choice in the matter.

Imagine their surprise to see a colorful, sanitary box of oatmeal--just the right size for a family supply--on the grocer's shelves. The new package caught on at once and it brought the housewife back for more Quaker Oats.

Now Harry had to work on distribution--getting supplies to the grocery stores to fill the demand created by his innovative packaging and marketing. Competition among the millers was fierce. Harry saw what was happening in other businesses through joint-ventures and trusts and saw an opportunity.

He went to some twenty other millers and suggested that they form a voluntary association of companies, with a single trade name, pricing, and marketing. He sat down and drafted the corporate policy of such an organization before taking it to the individual owners for ratification:

POLICY OF THE OATMEAL MILLERS ASSOCIATION OF OHIO

That we shall make better oatmeal and cereals of all kinds than has ever been manufactured.

That no matter what the cost, we will abandon systems and methods and scrap machinery whenever changes can be made for the improvement of quality, or lessoning of cost.

That we must not be dependent for volume or profit upon any one cereal, or country, or section of country; but to have our business so broadly distributed that panics or commercial disturbances or depressed times will not seriously cripple us or prevent our paying regular dividends.

That our selling organizations shall consist of men who are honest, intelligent, of good character, who are natural merchants and willing to render the very best service to the customers. Our purpose is not only to give the customers the very best of cereals, but to render to the jobbers and retailers a service that can not be equalled.

We are to scatter and diversify our business in all parts of the world, and do educational and constructive work so as to awaken an interest and create a demand for cereals where none existed. To this end, we will have no understandings, working arrangements or agreements with our competitors, but always keep ourselves in position to make any price that might be necessary to meet competition, should we want or need the business.

Harry read his statement to a group of mill owners who had come to hear his ideas. When he finished, he summarized his thoughts. "In short," he told them, "my policy has been to make better oatmeal and cereal of all kinds, to combine with other interested companies when there's mutual interest. I'm willing to take my chances to prove this idea will work. I'll put my company's assets into a separately chartered company with its own capital stock, central authority and a single trade name."

There were twenty millers in attendance who agreed to the plan. But one mill was conspicuous by its absence. Ferdinand Schumacher was suspicious of such a united effort.

Besides, Schumacher disliked Harry, calling him a brash young troublemaker.

"*Nein!*" he yelled out in his broken German when he was approached to join, "Why should I? I do not need you in my business! Keep your nose out of *mein* business."

So the twenty mills began under the umbrella of the *Oatmeal Millers Association* in an effort to combat the ruthless competition in the business and in order to maintain price stability, but it was happening without Schumacher's mill.

Because Schumacher's Jumbo Mill was so big, it had its own customers, inventory and staying power. He made his own rules for marketing his mill's production of oatmeal.

The old German miller was wise in the ways of production, inventory and market trends. He knew that nearly every spring, the early thaws turned the roads into nearly impassible muddy bogs. The mire kept delivery wagons from bringing grain to the mills for months, making oatmeal a scarce commodity until summer. So he stockpiled his grain for these times.

Schumacher had wisely built huge five-story bins beside his mill, enough to hold 100,000 bushels of oats--enough to not only carry him through the spring thaws, but a supply to last until the summer harvest. He was known in Akron as The Oatmeal King, and enjoyed the fame and attention of the name. After all, he *was* king. Schumacher was the largest single employer in Akron, the biggest buyer of goods, largest industrialist and greatest exporter. In fact, the entire local economy depended on the Jumbo Mill.

That was, however, until the night of March 6, 1886. The bells of the local church steeple had just struck two in the morning. There was still a raw, cold chill in the air. Suddenly the dark skies brightened. Flames began to rise from Schumacher's Jumbo Mill. As the night watchman ran for help, neighbors heard the commotion and the volunteer fire brigade was called out. But there was a lot of time lost in reporting the fire and getting help to fight the flames. The fire brigade finally brought the pumper up to a good head of steam and raced toward the mill, its team of four horses galloping madly, nostrils flaring and clouds of steam bellowing from their lungs.

By now, there was a large crowd watching the fire and the gapers almost blocked the pumper from getting through. Finally, the firefighters were on the scene. They played out the hoses and hooked them up to the pumper. But the equipment failed. Whether the water lines were frozen or something else was wrong, it didn't matter. The firemen were helpless when the pumper generated no pressure.

As the brigade worked on it, a call went out to a nearby town to send help. By now, the glow in the sky was seen as far away as Cleveland, over 30 miles away. Gamely, the nearby town of Kent sent its own fire pumper, but when it arrived, the hoses would not work because of a variation in the thread size in the hose attachments. Another pumper was put on a special train in Cleveland but it was derailed when the train struck a handcar on the tracks.

None of this would have mattered. By 3:00 A.M. the fire had already engulfed the Jumbo Mill--it was too late. The wooden frame of the mill incinerated explosively, fed by the highly combustible oats in the huge bins. By early dawn, Schumacher's pride and joy was totally wiped out. There was nothing left of even the foundation upon which he could rebuild. The fire left him in utter financial ruin.

Harry went to him right after the terrible fire. "I'm sorry, Ferdinand," he said. "If there's anything I can do, just let me know."

The German was humbled now, and didn't react violently to Harry as before. He simply told Harry the loss was so devastating because he had no insurance.

"No insurance!" Harry inquired incredulously. "Why?"

"*Ach*, they want such a fearful price for premiums. I wouldn't pay. But now--" He didn't have to finish his thought.

Before the fire, Schumacher had been selling 360,000 pounds of oatmeal *a day* to the retail grocery trade. Now there was nothing.

The Crowell Quaker Mill had undermined the sales of Jumbo Mill, even before the fire. After the fire, Schumacher's grocery customers received a letter from Crowell offering to provide them with the oatmeal that was previously supplied by the Jumbo Mill.

The Quaker product was not packaged in the big barrels as was Schumacher's oatmeal. Harry's product was packaged in customer-sized two pound packages, in vermin-proof boxes. Even before the fire, the Quaker Mill enjoyed a good business, and now--afterwards--business was booming. The grocers saw how much better the Quaker product was asked for and purchased by more customers than Schumacher's and so they switched suppliers. But Schumacher only saw the action as opportunistic, trying to put him out of business entirely.

However, Harry Crowell turned the other cheek and opened the door for the old German to get another chance. With Schumacher's business wiped out, Crowell's Quaker Mill could easily have put Jumbo Mill out of business for good. It would even have been a sound business decision. Harry could have wiped out a competitor and firmly established his own leadership and that of his company at the same time. Instead, he offered the old miller a second chance. Harry repeated his invitation to Schumacher to join the Association and rebuild with the encouragement of the other millers. "Maybe so," he said simply. "I will think about it and let you know."

Shortly after this, Schumacher sat across the desk from Harry in the offices of the Quaker Mill. Although Schumacher was a local giant, he was not a big man physically. Even before the disaster he hardly looked the part of industrial mogul. His dark, old clothes were ill-fitting and rumpled. His necktie was always twisted and quite worn at the knot, as if it were his only tie. He had a long, untrimmed beard and wide-brimmed hat that made him look more like an area farmer than the owner of a prosperous business and proclaimed leader of local society.

By contrast, Henry Parsons Crowell *did* look the part of chief executive of a major industry. He wore a tailored suit, tight-fitting in the Eastern fashion of the day. His celluloid collar was clean and white, with a finely knotted tie that looked new. He was not tall, about the same height as Schumacher, but somehow he had more stature. His face was clean shaven, except for a groomed mustache. His black hair was brushed into a careful style, parted down the middle and lightly oiled with barber cologne.

In appearance the two men were at opposite poles. So, too, were they opposite in personality and leadership style. Yet, for the first time, Schumacher was ready to listen to Henry Crowell talk about his becoming part of the Association with the other twenty millers. However, the German miller hadn't come hat in hand, as everyone expected.

Schumacher had shrewdly and quickly reorganized his business after the fire and had become almost as strong as before by somehow acquiring a local competitor, the *Akron Milling Company*. That company had little assets and only a small business base, but it had something of genuine value--a new oat-rolling mill that gave it more production capacity than many of the other mills combined. With it, Schumacher could once again compete.

When the Association had proposed a merger with Schumacher just after his fire, they expected he would be humbled and more reasonable. They were even willing to grant him the honor of having the company be named after him as a concession to his misfortune.

But far from being docile and cooperative, Schumacher bulldozed his way into the Association with a fierce determination to dictate new terms: he wanted a controlling interest based not on each mills' assets, but on production capacity (it's not certain the other millers knew yet that his

93

Akron Milling Company would be producing over half the total oatmeal production). As a second condition, Schumacher wanted no part of Henry Crowell being elected to any office in the company. Not only that, Schumacher proceeded to place most of his own family on the payroll as soon as he'd established his leadership.

But his dictatorial reign lasted only six months. By then, other mills had surpassed Schumacher in production and by using his own formula for determining shares of the company, he was unseated as the Association leader. But by now, many of the original milling companies were disillusioned and had dropped out. On May 4, 1887, the Association reorganized with seven of its largest member mills into a new company called the *Consolidated Oatmeal Company.*

The name of Henry Parsons Crowell was placed in nomination and he was elected president. His friend, Robert Stuart, was made managing vice-president. And Ferdinand Schumacher, used to running everything, was elected treasurer. They were now all equals.

Cranky old Schumacher couldn't stand having Henry Crowell as president, however. He said contemptuously, "It's stupid! Crowell knows absolutely nothing about this business. He's a troublesome newcomer with no experience in milling."

"But that's his strength," observed Robert Stuart. "That means he has no prejudices, no history or traditions to deal with, nobody to tell him his ideas won't work. You've got to admit, he's done his homework, though. And admit it or not, his ideas are innovative and practical."

"Humph!" Schumacher snorted.

Actually, Henry Crowell believed that God had led him to the Quaker Mill business. It was his conviction that this involvement was important and part of a greater stewardship with which he had been entrusted.

"No one, to my knowledge," said Stuart, "has ever approached a business venture as clear-minded and well-planned as Crowell." It was true. In the same way he had set out the policies, goals and objectives for the *Consolidated Oatmeal Company*, Henry Crowell had laid out a careful personal and business plan for establishing the *Quaker* brand name. He dealt with such futuristic concepts as a world market, of changing consumer habits, packaging, merchandising, advertising and the use of machinery and technology--years ahead of all others.

Henry had put his ideas into practice. His right hand man, Jim Andrews made them work in the mill. Their efficiency allowed them to undercut other companies in both price and quality. It established Quaker Mill once and for all. However, to Schumacher and most of Crowell's competitors, the ideas were strange, even grandiose. They thought his business and marketing schemes would fall apart in the real world when they were tested against traditional methods thought to be proven sound over the years.

They hadn't noticed--as Henry Crowell had--that their world was changing. Crowell was right; the way to produce and sell cereal did not lie in the antiquated methods that were a century or more out-of-date. Henry ignored their derision. The proof was in the results, and he had already proved that he was light years ahead of everyone else.

Chapter Nine

Henry concerned himself less with the intrigues and frustrations of the *Consolidated Cereal Company* and decided to wait for things to settle between Ferdinand Schumacher and himself. However, although his responsibilities as manager of *Consolidated Cereal* kept him busy, he was not totally occupied. Eventually, Henry became restless.

The winter snows of 1888 seemed particularly severe that year. They were not just harsh to those living in Ravenna, Ohio. All across the Midwest, and more particularly on the Great Plains, uncommonly terrible blizzards killed millions of cattle and other livestock on the farms and ranches. Cattlemen across the nation were wiped out. Their bankruptcies had lured foreign investors to come in and buy up what was left.

As Henry Crowell read about these incidents, he wondered about the big Percheron farm he had sold years earlier when he had gotten out of farming and ranching. This year, that decision seemed wise.

There were other disasters in the world that year. A global flu pandemic affected 40% of the world's population, and scores of millions died in America and overseas. Henry thought of Lillie, and her death from a similar illness. Their brief life together seemed such a distant memory now, yet he still missed the companionship.

His friends and co-workers noticed his melancholia and tried to interest him in other things. One friend seemed especially concerned. Ned Murfey had been hired by Henry as part of the Quaker Mill staff. The two were about the same age and a friendship formed immediately. The Murfeys had invited Henry to dinner so often that he seemed part of the family. In fact, they had even named one of their children Henry Parsons Murfey, after him.

In the loneliness after the death of Lillie, Henry had come to appreciate the company of this lively young family, and often dropped by for dinner or conversation.

One spring evening, after dinner, Rose Murfey interrupted the conversation of the two men talking shop in the parlor. "Henry, are you doing anything on Friday night?"

Henry looked up. "Uh, no. I don't think so. Why?"

"Well, a good friend of mine has just returned from overseas. She's been away on special study and is coming to Ravenna to visit me on Friday. I want her to stay for dinner, and would be pleased if you could come for dinner as well."

*   *   *   *

Rose Murfey told her husband later, after their guests had left, "Oh, Ned, it was love at first sight! Did you see the way they took to each other?"

"I sure did," Ned replied. "Why, did you hear--Henry even invited her to a concert in Cleveland on Sunday. What's it feel like to play Cupid?"

"*Ned!*" Rose blushed. "Was it that obvious? Do you think that Susan knew?"

Susan Coleman had lived across the street from Rose when the two of them grew up in Cleveland. They were life-long friends and Rose was certain that Susan would be charmed by the handsome widower.

And so it happened, some three years after Lillie's death, that Henry Crowell met and almost immediately fell in love with this woman of great charm and personality. At the Cleveland concert, Henry scarcely took his eyes off Susan. She was tall and quite pretty, with ivory skin and full red lips. Her hair was dark and swept up onto her head after the style of the day. Her grey eyes were round and soft.

Henry watched as Susan enjoyed the music, her eyes welling up with emotion when the instruments played. He saw her chest rise and fall excitedly during the orchestra's final passionate crescendo and climax. Her appreciation of music and arts bordered almost on ardor.

After the concert they drove the carriage back to Susan's home. Stopping at a crossroads, Henry called, "Whoa, Susan!"

Startled, the young woman seated beside him jumped. "What!?" she exclaimed.

"Not you," Henry chuckled. "My horse. That's *her* name, and I've known her longer than I've known you."

They laughed together and continued their drive. Henry learned from Susan that she was an 1882 graduate of Vassar College. Her interests in college, apart from academics, were in the fields of art, drama, literature along with the usual round of social activities. Following her graduation from Vassar, Susan moved to Detroit where she taught Latin and math in Liggett School. After teaching for several years, she spent time in Cleveland, then took a year off to study in Europe. In fact, Susan had only recently returned from Germany when she first visited her childhood friend, Rose Murfey.

Henry was smitten not just by Susan Coleman's beauty and personality. He was quite impressed with her wit and intelligence, and by her amazing grasp of business. Women of the day generally seemed uninterested in business, and left such talk to their husbands. But Susan was not only interested, but frequently offered her opinions or suggestions on improving a work-related method or solving a problem.

At one of their frequent dinners at the Murfey home, Henry told Susan about his concern for his younger brother, Charles, who was troubled with the same illness which had incapacitated Henry for so many years.

"Charlie has to give up his business and go West for his health," Henry told her. "I wish I could find someone to take over his business and run it until Charlie is recovered."

"I know just the person!" Susan exclaimed. "In fact, I've been wanting to introduce him to you for some time."

"Really?"

"Yes. His name is Frank Drury, and he has an invention to market. I told him to see you about it. I've seen it and I think it has real possibilities."

Drury met with Susan and Henry later that week. He brought with him a prototype of the invention Susan had described. He explained how it all came about.

"Six years ago, I was a clerk in a hardware store in Cleveland. There was this old Swede, a tinsmith who came into the store one day with this thing, all wrapped up with newspaper. He showed it to the owner and asked if he wanted to buy more of these contraptions to sell in his store."

Drury took the sample out of its wrapping and set it out on the table.

"What is it?" Henry asked.

"The old Swede--the fella who invented it--called it a 'lamp stove'. See, its a simple device, about the size of a table lamp but with a larger kerosene reservoir--here." His finger pointed out the various components as he talked. "And see, it's got a much bigger wick than a lamp. This top frame is riveted on, and it's strong enough for the person to set a pot or pan on top of it and cook."

Intrigued, Henry examined the lamp stove. "And what's your role in this?"

As Drury sat down, his excitement and enthusiasm were obvious. "The owner of the store bought then sold out every lamp stove the inventor brought us. He's making them over at Taylor and Boggis, you know--that little foundry across town. Well, I went to Taylor and told him that the two of us ought to build and market this remarkable invention. I said, 'Let's buy the rights, get a patent, and make these stoves ourselves.' But he said, "No, thanks. I think I'll just leave well enough alone.' I guess he felt he was making enough money just filling orders for the old Swede. But I just can't seem to let it alone."

Henry nodded, his own imagination captured now.

Susan added, "Henry, you've told me how you're out to change the breakfast habits of the country with your oatmeal. Well, I started to think. More and more people are moving from the farms into the cities. Many of them live in tiny apartments with no room for a big kitchen wood stove. This lamp stove is simple, and really efficient."

Drury gave Henry some papers on which he'd worked out the financial prospects for this venture. He showed the expenses, and projections for sales of the units. "If you'll put up the capital," he told Henry, "I'll manage it and do the selling. We can be partners."

The partnership was sealed with a handshake and not long after, Henry and Frank Drury completed incorporation papers, bought the old buildings of a defunct factory, and started their own foundry for making lamp stoves. The enterprise, *Cleveland Foundry Company*, soon began building and selling their *Perfection Stoves*.

In this, as in so many other ways, Susan Coleman was a surprising breath of fresh air to Henry, and an answer to his lingering loneliness. Soon, they were spending almost all of their free time together. It was truly a whirlwind courtship, but each of them had the assurance that they had found their destined soul mate. Their engagement was announced in early summer, and they were married on July 10, 1888, in the Cleveland home of Susan's parents.

*   *   *   *

The offices of *Consolidated Cereal Company* were moved to Chicago, so Henry and his new bride, Susan, moved there in the fall of 1888. Henry could hardly believe the transformation of the city since his visits during his train trips to the West.

There were skyscrapers everywhere, and brand new elevated trains were running through the entire downtown area, providing quick transportation for all.

Three years later, the *Consolidated Oatmeal Company* was reorganized. The members had agreed to combining their assets in a merger so they could be a single, viable company, as Henry Crowell had advocated. The new company would be called *American Cereal Company* and all were agreeable to the merger terms except Schumacher. He had, in his usual shrewd fashion, held out so he could transfer all of his intangible as well as tangible assets as part of the merger, the result gave him 50% ownership and control of the stock. The Crowell and Stuart shares represented just 12% each. The former oatmeal king had regained his throne.

Now it was a battle between generations. Schumacher stubbornly resented the new-fangled and untried ideas of Henry Crowell. He couldn't imagine why anyone would want to change the way things were done. Henry actively promoted his concepts and showed how and why they were superior to the present methods. But the old man was threatened by the young up-start (as he called him).

Schumacher had voting control, so he immediately unseated Henry as president and voted himself in as chairman. Henry became a vice president and general manager. Robert Stuart became secretary-treasurer. The minority shareholders considered selling out, but decided to stick with it, reasoning that since Schumacher had approved the way Henry's partner, Jim Andrews, ran the plant, at least the innovations already introduced would not be tossed out. They also thought that with Stuart as treasurer, he could help keep Schumacher's spending under control--even if he couldn't keep his relatives off the payroll.

Despite the friction between its owners, the *American Cereal Company* made fantastic profits over the next several years. Even during the depression of 1893, many were fearful of new start-ups like *American Cereal*. It was the worst financial panic in decades. Some 600 banks failed; 74 railroads went under; over 15,000 other businesses declared bankruptcy and European investors created even more panic by dumping their American investments. When silver prices collapsed, and the depression hung on, people everywhere were fearful.

But *American Cereal's* Quaker Oats proved to be a depression-proof commodity. Even in the terrible economic times, sales exploded. The company was so successful that it was even able to buy its chief competitor when it ran into financial difficulty during the 1893 depression.

Reluctantly, Schumacher also had to accept Henry's innovative packaging concepts. Sales of the attractive red-blue-and-yellow boxes with the Quaker man and name on the front far outdistanced anything like that of the old days.

Henry pushed for budget to not only package Quaker Oats in sanitary, colorful and individually sized boxes, but for money to spend on advertising to convince customers why this was a better choice than a sack of oatmeal from the unsanitary barrel in the grocery and why customers should continue buying Quaker Oats after trying them.

At this Schumacher hit the ceiling. "I've said this before, but nobody wants to listen! That's money that comes out of *our* pockets. It's crazy to spend money to change our packaging to a box instead of a barrel. Who cares about it? But to spend even *more* money to advertise, I say, leave well enough alone. The grocers don't want boxes, and the people don't either. And advertising is crazy. Let our competitors advertise--it'll put 'em out of business sooner!"

The old man had other stockholders thinking as he did. Henry had a difficult task, but finally convinced the owners to spend money to advertise the Quaker product. Such an idea was revolutionary. After all, the primary advertising of the day consisted mostly of untrue claims for spurious products. "Snake oil peddlers," Schumacher had called them, and rightly so. Most ads were false and misleading pitches for patent medicines, inventions and confidence schemes.

No one knew what might happen if someone tried to sell a legitimate product with honest claims. Yet, Henry approached the challenge with the same kind of deliberate thinking he had given to his other ventures. "First," he told his colleagues, "we must convince our customers that they *need* our cereal. And they do. In this depression, housewives don't have money to buy beef. So, how do they feed their families and give them the vitamins and other essential elements for their children to stay healthy and grow? Our Quaker Oats need to be foremost on the minds of mothers everywhere. If we put handbills on every telegraph pole, billboards on every barn, signs on every wagon and advertisements in every magazine and newspaper in America, it won't be long before *everyone* will be asking for Quaker Oats!"

Crowell's proposals carried weight because he had already shown how people responded at his earlier promotions. Taking a cue from his *Percheron Parade* that had so electrified farmers from Ohio to North Dakota who saw the great billboards on the box cars of his special train, Henry had created colorful billboards for freight cars taking crates of Quaker Oats across America. These had a huge picture of a box of cereal with the man in Quaker garb, with the words: *Quaker Oats, the World's Breakfast.*

"That's what has generated such fantastic sales," Henry told them. "Do you think that mothers in Kansas just one day wake up and think, 'Perhaps there's a new oatmeal in a box with the name, Quaker Oats, on it. I'll go to the grocer and ask him for it.' Product awareness doesn't ever happen automatically, gentlemen. It has to be created. That's why we must advertise."

Schumacher continued to fight Henry's advertising and marketing ideas tooth and nail, but for the most part, Henry prevailed. His advertising did prove effective. One early advertisement showed a picture of a beautiful young baby, sure to get any mother's attention while reading the newspaper. A catchy headline: *Always the Best Food* captured the reader's attention. The copy then explained that a dime's worth of oatmeal was more healthful than a dollar's worth of meat, and how that could be--showing the benefits of Quaker Oats--and telling the reader to ask for the product by name, thus building brand awareness and loyalty.

Henry researched and wrote the ads himself. And they were effective. Soon, the *Quaker* name and trademark image were universally visible. They were painted on barns, box cars, wagons, and even street cars. Metal signs were nailed to fence posts, telegraph poles, grocery screen doors and windows. There were display ads in newspapers, magazines and on posters pasted everywhere. And calendars, blotters, free premiums and cookbooks, mailing stuffers.

There was simply no escaping Henry's efforts to make *Quaker* a name on everyone's lips. He felt that advertising was effective only as it gave constant exposure to the product. He pioneered the use of celebrity testimonials and endorsements to prove value. Henry also invented contests and prizes requiring the mailing in of a box top, did market testing and provided a heavy stream of sample products to give away at fairs, train stations, ball games and other places where crowds convened. All are from the Crowell mind and creativity, although many are surprised, thinking such inventions were from a modern-day ad agency.

The genius of Henry's advertising and promotion is summed up in what it accomplished. Quaker Oats' success came because they sold a good product, to be sure. But what helped it sell was its distinctive colorful cardboard box. It was something that was difficult for competitors to copy and far too expensive to replace or change methods of distribution.

The box itself even became an advertisement of sorts. On the box was printed this advisory to the housewife:

We would call your special attention to the purity, rapidity
of preparation, and the fact that they did not sacrifice
sweetness and flavor for the sake of rapid cooking.

So the box not only touted the sanitary freshness of the
product, it even gave a fool-proof recipe for making the cereal.
There were other recipes--for fried pudding, pancakes, Quaker
bread--and instructions for straining oatmeal into infant food.

Before Henry Crowell reinvented advertising, taking it
away from patent medicine charlatans, most print ads were used
to convince grocers to buy and inventory your product. If the
grocer sold it, he might re-order. But now, Henry completely
bypassed that inefficient and unreliable system. He addressed his
advertising to the consumer, not the grocer, and told consumers
why they needed his product.

He used brief, pointed messages to convince people:
One pound of Quaker Oats makes as much bone
and muscle as three pounds of beef.
Is it worth trying?

In the old days, salesmen also sold product directly to
the stores. If they were high-pressure salesmen, more often than
not the storekeepers ended up with more product than they
could easily sell. It sat in the big open barrels that spoiled or
became vermin-infested.

Henry's method by-passed the storekeeper completely
and reversed the salesmen's high pressure tactics. It was
housewives who pressured the grocer when he didn't have
Quaker Oats on the shelves when they came to buy. Then the
grocer had no resistance for an advance demand of the product.
It insured quick rotation of his inventory, while his sales
continued to climb.

Yet, despite the successful advertising resulting in sales
that went through the roof year after year, Schumacher never
relented. It was as if every dollar for advertising, promotion or
marketing was being wrenched from the old man's own purse.

It was truly a battle of two competing philosophies and business approaches.

Schumacher detested philosophies and presented with great passion his own ideas and the traditions and methods of the 19th century, while Henry Crowell and Robert Stuart pointed to the 20th century and embraced ideas that would lead the company into the future.

Ferdinand Schumacher, tired and feeling his age, thought his own leadership was being ridiculed by every success of the men who ought to have been his colleagues, but in his mind, they were his enemies. He didn't trust these younger men. They were, after all, the same age as his sons, and he reasoned, if his sons were still so immature and useless, then these other men must be as well.

So, despite the success of the business, old man Schumacher began to think of possible ways of getting rid of his two junior partners.

Chapter Ten

Henry Crowell was not concerned about Ferdinand Schumacher. He believed that things would eventually be righted within the company; that sooner or later, the other shareholders would come to their senses and follow him. Besides, Henry was already a well known business giant, famous for his efforts in making Quaker Oats a household name--every bit as eminent as Kellogg or Post. As a result, Schumacher had no leverage in trying to make Henry bend his principles.

Nor did Henry need the money he was being paid to manage the company and handle its advertising. His earlier start-up of the *Perfection Stove* foundry had proved to be sound. Sales began slowly but began to grow. Following the strategies he'd invented at the cereal company, he and Frank Drury sold enough stoves in the years leading up to the new century to make each of them a millionaire.

Despite the depression which had begun at the early part of the decade, *American Cereal* continued to enjoy growing sales. Henry knew the increased sales, due in large part from the Quaker Oats business, were because of his advertising budget. But Schumacher took exception to this and tried to convince the other shareholders that there'd have been another $400,000 in operating profit for them to share if money hadn't been "squandered" on Crowell's advertising.

Then a crisis occurred. The tight financial situation caused by the depression and the company's heavy costs in Europe, along with Henry's $500,000 ad budget, caused a cash flow shortage in the company. This was followed by a sales slump. Treasurer Robert Stuart, for the first time in the company's operating history, was faced with a quarterly loss. This gave Schumacher the ammunition he was looking for and he demanded Stuart's resignation.

Henry went to his friend's defense, arguing that the crisis was temporary and an increase in business had already wiped out that earlier operating deficit. Not only that, the company had an operating profit of over $300,000 for the year.

But it was too late. The board of directors fired Stuart, agreeing with Schumacher that there truly was a financial crisis. Yet, it was not enough of a crisis to prevent them from declaring a double dividend for shareholders.

The situation proved that Schumacher had the votes to not only make life miserable for Henry and Stuart. Now, without his friend to give him strength and encouragement, Henry's position was also being undermined, and it wouldn't be long before Schumacher would find a cause for eliminating Henry Crowell. However, since Henry Crowell was a powerful man in his own right, both in and out of the company, Schumacher was careful to avoid a "once and for all" battle with Henry. Nor did Henry challenge Schumacher when his advertising budget was cut by almost 20% by Schumacher's directors. A brief truce was in effect.

Still, Schumacher was confused and frustrated. With such a position of outside strength and wealth, it seemed unreasonable to him that Henry Crowell would want to keep his position of General Manager. Yet, Henry was not about to give up his role in the company and watch it be wiped out without completely testing his ideas about advertising and marketing of brand name foods. His stubborn refusal to sell out or leave the company only angered the old German more than ever.

Robert Stuart, meanwhile, had taken a position with the American National Bank in Chicago and made a smooth transition into the new role. One September day in 1897, he was visited by Henry Crowell and another man who was introduced as Mr. Swift.

"I'll get right to the point," Swift began. "I'm a corporation attorney and we've learned that Schumacher plans to call for Henry's resignation at the next board meeting. I think we must write to the shareholders, to them directly with our case and try and get their proxies. Otherwise, it's hopeless-- Schumacher has a majority of shares and can do as he pleases."

Henry added, "Between us, Robert, we own 24% of the shares in *American Cereal.* We simply can't sit by and let Schumacher toss us aside."

"Well, the real reason he wanted me out was to install his son, Hugo, as treasurer. Now there's no one there to veto the old man's 'appointments' of cronies and family members to the board or put them on the payroll," observed Stuart.

"We must try," urged Crowell. "What he's doing isn't right. It must be opposed."

Their letter to shareholders was followed by a scathing letter from Schumacher and his hand-picked directors. He reminded stockholders that his own control of the company was absolute and that Crowell was the culprit. "There can never be peace," he said, "as long as one man claims the right to be absolutely a dictator."

Just after New Year's day in 1897, Henry wrote another letter. This time, he laid out all the facts of Robert Stuart's dismissal, accusing Schumacher of inventing false charges in order to get rid of Stuart. Henry also listed all the cronies and family members put on the payroll or board of directors which he and Stuart had believed to be wrong. And simply because of his concern for the company, Robert Stuart was unfairly dismissed.

Henry also reminded the stockholders that because of Stuart's careful financial management and his own advertising and marketing plans, the company had prospered --even during the depression. Schumacher countered this letter with charges of his own--(lies actually)--saying that Stuart had plotted to drive the company stock down so he and relatives could buy it at a discount.

In mid-February the annual meeting took place in an atmosphere of highly charged emotions. Schumacher got right to the point.

"We now have on hand, ready to vote, much more than a majority," he told them. He nodded in the direction of the other directors who had sided with him in this struggle. "We absolutely and unqualifiedly refuse to serve with Mr. Crowell on the Board of Directors," he stormed.

As he continued to rage at Crowell, and by manipulating the financial picture, he told shareholders of a good profit which he had generated, more proof that Stuart and Crowell were holding back the company.

One of Schumacher's directors listened with keen interest. Will Christy, the Cleveland banker whom the wily Schumacher had put on the board to bolster his own reputation among bankers, curiously paid attention to Henry's position. He had been convinced of Schumacher's position against Henry Crowell before the meeting. But now, he wasn't so certain.

Crowell seemed to him to be a reasonable man with a clear understanding of the cereal business and its operations.

But when the vote was taken, Henry Crowell was unseated from the Board. When that happened, Jim Andrews-- the genius behind the company's production--also resigned. Now Schumacher was almost gleeful. He alone was left to operate *American Cereal* without confrontations with the financial controls of Stuart, the advertising expenses and constant challenges of Crowell. His only discomfort was that he was now also without the technical wizardry of Andrews, Crowell's partner and friend.

With the elimination of Stuart, Crowell and Andrews, Schumacher's competitors saw what was happening, even if he himself did not. Some 13 independent millers formed their own association to go head-to-head with *American Cereal* and challenge the superiority of Quaker Oats in the marketplace.

Henry saw this as both a challenge and an opportunity. There was no way that Schumacher could maintain the growth of the company without the three key men who were themselves responsible for its success. It would only be a matter of time before it began to show up on the balance sheet where it might give Henry more credibility among the other stockholders. But by then it might be too late--some new competitor could overwhelm the company before Henry could help it regain its equilibrium and sales superiority.

From his stove company headquarters in Chicago, Henry was in telephone contact with Robert Stuart, and the two of them spent the better part of the year thinking of ways to battle Schumacher and regain the company. The problem was, how to get controlling interest away from the old man. Schumacher and his family controlled 17,000 of the 34,262 shares outstanding--slightly less than 50% but enough for control of the company.

Henry and Stuart decided to buy up as many shares as they could, starting with a group in New England willing to sell

3,400 shares. Other sources--64 shares from Iowa, 600 shares in Ohio--the latter source a shirt-tail relation to Schumacher, gave the two men encouragement.

About the same time, there were others who saw the opportunity to take control of *American Cereal*. A group of Cleveland stock speculators began to buy up shares through a Chicago financier. The men were being fed inside information from Will Christy, the banker appointed by Schumacher to the Board. Christy saw that Schumacher was inept, a man in over his head. Upon more serious consideration, Christy saw that it was Crowell and Stuart, along with Jim Andrews, who were really responsible for the success of the company, making it paramount in the industry in less than half a decade. And if this success were to continue, it would have to be with these ousted directors put back in charge.

*   *   *   *

The speculators called Henry Crowell and Robert Stuart to Cleveland for a secret meeting with their spokesman, Myron T. Herrick, a highly visible financier and rising political star. The men were told of the plan to seize the company. But the plans went far beyond what Henry had envisioned.

"We'll have a company that'll have enough capital to not only buy up *American Cereal*," Herrick told them. "But then we'll buy out or squeeze out all the other independent mills, all the competition! We'll end up with the most powerful cereal trust in the world. We'll have absolute control of pricing, distribution, everything."

Henry glanced at Stuart. His friend had said nothing, but he sensed that he, too, saw this as going in the wrong direction. The two men listened but were non-committal in their response. Yet, they left the door open for the speculators to support them in a proxy fight to oust Schumacher.

The Cereal Tycoon

The old German was unruffled by the activity of stock buying, which now could not be kept secret. Ironically, when he saw Cleveland bankers and speculators buying his company's stock, he was not concerned. He had discreetly looked into it and learned that they were buying at the suggestion of Will Christy. His logical assumption was that any friends of Christy's were also allies of Schumacher. Besides, the buying was forcing up the value of the stock.

When Henry and the speculators began buying the stock, it was selling at $40, then $50 a share. Within a few weeks, it had climbed to $95 a share. Delighted at the prospects of a windfall, Schumacher decided to sell a small amount of his shares--to pick up some of the profit, and to help pay off a business debt from another of his holdings. *Not to worry,* he thought, *because Will Christy's friends own the other shares.*

After Schumacher sold 3,000 shares of his own stock he no longer had the majority of the outstanding shares--and thus controlling interest. The speculators, along with Christy and Herrick, announced that their syndicate was supporting Crowell and Stuart--a fatal blow to the old German's rule.

When news reached Schumacher, he slumped into his office chair felling ill and shaken, beaten by the "upstart" Crowell, Ferdinand Schumacher finally gave up. He was 73, and unable to rebound from this calamity. He knew it was over.

When the word reached the stock market, the clear purpose of the speculators was known, as well as the knowledge of Schumacher's loss of absolute control. The stock immediately fell back to $40 a share. But the shrewd old man knew enough to hang on to his remaining shares until the syndicate finally bought out the shares owned by him and his family for $95 a share.

Only then did Ferdinand Schumacher retire from *American Cereal.*

*   *   *   *

Just before the annual meeting of the stockholders in 1899, the news was released that the syndicators had formed a holding company with a war chest of $33 million to consolidate all cereal interests into a giant trust. This was ten times the asset value of the company, even at $95 a share.

As major investors in the company, the speculators took a major step toward their intentions by putting the name of Myron Herrick on the ballot for Chairman of the Board at the February annual meeting of the stockholders. Herrick was voted in as Chairman, replacing the retired and exiled Schumacher, and as his first order of business, he proposed that Henry Crowell be named the new president and Robert Stuart be elected treasurer. Then he called on Crowell to present his business plan. Henry was expected to ratify the trust deal and ask for a vote to have *American Cereal* join the holding company as part of the trust.

Instead, Henry gave a presentation that first reviewed the history of the company under the leadership of its capable founding directors (without impugning his old enemy, Schumacher). Then he outlined a case for *not* proceeding with the plans to join the trust.

"We've heard about the benefits to our company by joining this new holding company which proposes to buy not just our company, but all the other cereal producers and millers as well. Their rationale is that it will control costs, limit competition and allow unlimited pricing. Well, that's the nature of a trust," Henry told them. "And here's why we believe it is wrong."

He spoke eloquently and authoritatively, reminding the shareholders that he felt such a move was morally wrong, that such a trust flew in the face of the ethic which had given America its greatness. And, looking at it with a more practical view, it was just the kind of activity that the government "trust busters" wanted to put out of business.

Henry, backed by financial plans prepared by his friend and new treasurer of the company, presented a well-defined rationale for moving the business ahead with the business plan that had worked so well in the past. Henry concluded his presentation with a convincing argument.

"If we are to proceed down this other path, I am afraid for our stockholders. Our profits will be eaten up by attorney fees and other huge costs of litigation and in contending with the government. And how would we defend ourselves against these trust charges? Because we certainly *will* be a monopoly. I believe the government is just waiting for the syndicate to go ahead with this plan so the U. S. Attorney General can bring them up on charges of trying to manipulate the market. The federal government is already on record as saying that monopolies are unfair and illegal. This is my belief as well, so it is not a path upon which I will lead you. I will *not* bring the matter to you for a vote," Henry told them.

Looking around the big meeting room, he looked for a response. There was unusual quiet acceptance and even some nodding of agreement. Henry looked to Chairman Herrick, who--after all--was the organizing mind behind the syndicate. It really didn't matter what the other shareholders thought--he had the votes to carry the matter if a motion was put forth by the Chairman.

It had been the stated purpose of the investors from the start to move forward toward a monopolistic trust because that's where they'd earn the most money. Henry expected an even larger conflict now with the syndicate than any he'd previously faced with Schumacher. Surely Herrick would not stand for Crowell's bold opposition. As Henry watched, the Chairman's expression had not changed, and Henry had no idea of his thoughts until he spoke.

For a long time, Herrick was silent. Then, slowly he rose to his feet.

"Thank you, Mr. Crowell," he said in a low voice. He paused before saying any more, then looked across the crowd and continued speaking. "Gentlemen, this is quite a turn of events, I must say."

Henry did not shrink from his stand and his body language told the audience that he would not recant. Herrick stared at him for a long moment, then abruptly turned to face the shareholders.

"Yes, indeed. It is quite a turn of events. But listening to Mr. Crowell, I found myself agreeing with everything he said about the--uh--*ethical* considerations being proposed. He has made a convincing argument against the trust deal. In fact, his point regarding the potential problems and the high costs in fighting the government are even more persuasive than his--uh--moral objections to it. In any event, it is up to him to put the matter before you for a vote. And I take by his comments that Mr. Crowell will not be making that proposal today. So, I say the matter, for now, is tabled. And if there is no further business, may I entertain a motion that our annual stockholders meeting be adjourned?"

For several weeks after the meeting, the Cleveland investors persisted, trying to get Henry and his associates to reconsider their opposition to the trust deal. Then they gave up. The deal fell through. The investors went on to other ventures and the newly elected leaders of *American Cereal* went about their business of restoring the company to its position of leadership. Henry and Robert Stuart were now free to move quickly into the new realm of establishing Quaker on their terms and on a global level. They started first in Great Britain, then moved to other foreign markets and built a strong demand for the Quaker brand name.

*   *   *   *

115

Some time later, Henry took time to reflect. He prayed with special gratitude to God for protecting him, guiding him and keeping his motives and actions pure during the long years of struggle to keep his company.

Faith. That's what it was, pure and simple. Henry was reminded of the verse, *"Without faith it is impossible to please God."* But he also knew something should be said for perseverance, too. Words from his school days at Greylock had guided his actions: *Take your time . . . and find the will of God.* Godly perserverance had helped him. It was neither easy nor quick. From the time Henry had first heard about and bought the Quaker Mill until now, twenty long years had passed.

A generation, he thought. *An entire generation has been born and come of age in the time it's taken to regain control of my company!* A great one for careful plans and thoughtful policies, Henry decided to establish some controls so that this kind of battle would never happen again. He reorganized the company, naming it after the world-famous brand name that had helped it become a giant industry. The *American Cereal Company* became the Quaker Oats Company, which was set up as the holding company for a number of other of its various products and companies.

In order to safeguard control of the company, Henry, with his friend, Robert Stuart and others, formed a special trust. In it, they assigned over 20,000 shares of voting stock in the new company. The trust was pledged to vote in concert with the management at the annual meetings, giving them perpetual control.

The Quaker Oats Company quadrupled its assets in just a few years, proving the soundness of returning Crowell and Stuart (and Jim Andrews) to power. Even the syndicate investors who had wanted to create a cereal conglomerate were agreeable to being bought out. A $1.2 million bond was set up to repay them for the stock they had purchased to get rid of Schumacher. This bond was completely retired in seven years.

Henry Crowell became known as the man who changed American breakfast habits. He had seen in the lowly oat grain a healthy and nutritious food and set about creating a world market for Quaker Oats. By 1908, the Quaker trademark was known by more people in more countries than any other brand on any kind of goods in the entire world.

His advertising was a model for the industry, but more than that, it became the standard for other new businesses. Henry watched as something else was emerging: advertising agencies that specialized in the kind of services he had created. No one who travelled could go far without seeing a Quaker Oats billboard painted on a barn or on the side of brick building. Bus cards, posters, and handbills were everywhere. Quaker ads were in the *Saturday Evening Post, Colliers,* and other national periodicals.

He used new technology to create other foods--and introduced them with the same flair as he had introduced Percheron horses to farmers on the northern plains.

As Henry reflected over the accomplishments of the past decades, he gave thanks for the way that God had brought him through it all. And, although satisfied with his material success, he felt there was still a void in his life. Perhaps it was time for more introspection and reflection to discover what made him incomplete.

Chapter Eleven

Henry Crowell determined that the thing missing from his life was a sense that all that he was doing, he was doing for God. True, God had kept His part of a promise that a much younger Harry Crowell had made after hearing evangelist D. L. Moody--that if he were allowed to make money, he'd make sure that God would receive the glory.

Now, Henry thought more about that compact. Surely God had already blessed him with an abundance of riches. And since the beginning, even as a boy, he had tithed his income--a lesson his father taught him well before he died. However, as Henry's wealth increased, so did the size of his tithe. No longer content to give just ten percent, his contributions towards God's work went up each year--to as much as 70% of his income in later years, a trend that continued for another 40 years. Yet, even the satisfaction of his "super" tithing did not give him the sense of peace and assurance he sought.

Henry and Susan had joined Fourth Presbyterian Church in Chicago after their marriage and move to the city in the fall of 1888. Ten years later, when Henry had been temporarily voted out of his company, they lived comfortably at 167 Rush Street, within walking distance of the church.

It was also near the Moody Bible Institute. Several years earlier, D. L. Moody had met with William Newell, a 28-year-old minister from Ohio. Moody told Newell that the MBI faculty had met and wanted him to be the superintendent of the Bible Institute. Part of the job responsibilities included his being available on weekends to speak in other cities. Newell's new wife, Millicent, was left behind in Chicago, and so she joined Fourth Presbyterian and attended there in her husband's absence.

It was at Fourth Presbyterian Church that Millicent met Susan Crowell. The young women became close friends and often met for companionship and to compare notes on their famous husbands. Each was also a young mother of a baby boy, so the two had even more to visit about when they got together.

It was Susan who came up with an idea when Henry had been sharing his vague uneasiness about his spiritual life.

"Darling, why don't we have a Bible study in our home. Millicent's husband is a famous Bible teacher. We could invite your business friends, or people from church," she suggested.

It wasn't exactly what Henry had in mind, but he could think of no reason they should *not* do it. So, beginning in the fall of 1889, Dr. Newell came to the Crowell's Rush Street home to conduct a weekly Bible study.

Newell and Henry found they had common spiritual and intellectual interests and they soon became friends who met on a more personal level, sharing each other's concerns and plans. Henry was totally absorbed by his new friend's knowledge of God's Word. Even though he had read the Bible regularly since childhood, when he prayed for health and direction for his life, Henry used Scriptures more for devotional inspiration than specific day-to-day guidance.

The studies in the Crowell home were remarkable for two unique events, if for no others. First, Susan Crowell was soundly converted. She had met and married Henry with a strong tradition of religious background. In her world, religion consisted of the major rituals and traditions of the church--infant christening, confirmation, marriage, and eventually a fine eulogy and burial sermon. And of course, whenever possible, a fine and inspiring Sunday service.

During these occasions, though, Susan Crowell had never considered that much of what she had been exposed to in church was more social than religious.

Now, Susan was brought face to face with sharp principles as Dr. Newell presented studies in the book of

Romans from the New Testament. She learned about sin and salvation, about the power of the indwelling Holy Spirit. Dr. Newell's lessons absolutely transformed Susan Crowell. She changed from a nominal Christian to a dynamic disciple, on fire for her Lord.

Susan's conversion not only changed her life, it was the talk of the so-called *Gilded 400*, Chicago's official list of wealthy, famous and infamous society families. Because of her transformation, Susan's life made a 180 degree turn. Things she had previously permitted in her life or home were not allowed anymore. In place of the insipid society balls or parties, Susan's life now revolved around her church and in helping people. Matrons of the *Gilded 400* felt uncomfortable in her presence and looked for ways to gracefully drop the Crowells from their guest lists. Why, who knows, if you invited the Crowells, they might start talking to people about God right on the spot!

Henry was certainly not bothered by such snubs. He was totally energized by his wife's conversion, too. Her life had been dramatically changed by the experience, and their young son, Henry Coleman Crowell, was chief beneficiary. Susan poured herself into his young life and gave him a solid, biblical upbringing.

Something every bit as dynamic happened to Henry as well as Susan. Dr. Newell's Bible studies helped Henry turn his life around, too. It couldn't be said that he was "born again" as was Susan, because he had been twice born when he received Christ into his life as a ten-year-old in his pastor's study.

But Henry found something for which he had been praying--something to fill that void in his spiritual life. It was more like Henry Crowell, at 43, had turned another corner, moving from recognition as "Christian businessman" to "Christian statesman".

As Henry and Susan began to exercise their Christianity, Henry began to take a more aggressive role in sharing his faith in business circles as well. One day, he was having lunch at the prestigious Union League Club with a prominent Chicago business leader, William Robinson. Robinson recalls sitting at a table beneath the Lincoln portrait, listening to Henry Crowell tell him about Jesus Christ.

He reported on the meeting later, "One by one my objections fell away. Henry was quite persuasive. I decided, then and there, as I would answer any corporation question, to come to God. From that day I have been a new creature in Christ Jesus . . . all my doubts, skepticism . . . were swept away. My swearing stopped. I went back to my office and told my closest associate. He listened to what had happened to me, and he grasped my hand and told me, 'I want that, too. I'll start with you!'"

There were other corporation giants who came to Christ after meeting with Henry Crowell. He was now finding his life was more satisfying, and the void he had prayed about a few years earlier was now being filled.

Henry recognized something else was shaping itself in his consciousness. It was a credo of sorts. His only other credo had been to make money--as much for God's purposes as his own, of course--but now he saw a different set of priorities that had as much to do with his personal stewardship as his making money and his "super" tithing.

There was a three-tiered aspect of his stewardship that Henry began to feel was important to God, and consequently to him and Susan. He wondered, if he'd let God into the planning and use of his time, as he had done with his money, could that dimension of his life also be increased in millionaire proportions?

As he thought about it, Henry divided his stewardship into three categories: first, of course, was the stewardship of his *money*, the most obvious area. By now, God had blessed him with such great wealth that it took much prayer, evaluation and thought to know how and where to use it.

There were others, of course, who would be quite happy to help Henry spend his money. Each week the mail brought a number of letters soliciting him for help. Some were honest requests for works of Christian integrity. Some, though, were thinly disguised requests from freeloaders for a handout. One writer apparently believed that it was always much easier to be generous with someone else's money. He wrote: *Give all your money away at once. Communism is coming. Give your money away before it is confiscated!* That writer even included a suggestion or two as to whom Henry might give away his money. Guess who was to be an important beneficiary!

More than a hundred Christian organizations were the real beneficiaries of the Crowell stewardship. Henry poured huge amounts of money into those he most believed in and which were doing real work with his contributions. There would eventually be millions of dollars donated to worthy causes: missions and missionaries, churches, prison ministries, tract publication, Bible translation work and printing, Bible helps in foreign languages, medical missions, help for the poor, for orphans and widows, money for medical bills for those in need, loans to young people who wanted an education but couldn't afford one--this list is nearly endless.

A contribution from his tithing could quite easily rescue an ailing ministry like Moody Bible Institute. Or, a more modest gift of $10,000 (modest for his ability to give) as a donation for a missionary would in no way stretch Henry's purse--but it could have such an impact on the missionary that he might not recover.

Or, the recipient might take Henry's generosity for granted and not work toward a long term solution to his problems. Without the testing of faith to find funding, a missionary might spend money in the wrong ways or be distracted by the size of the gift. Henry reasoned that he must be careful with his contributions. Too much money might create as many problems as not enough.

The stewardship of his money was something Henry Crowell learned early on. His father had set an example that had indelibly impressed him with his obligation to give back a portion of the fruits of his labor. He also learned from his own experience that it was impossible to outgive God.

The more money Henry gave to Christian causes, the more God blessed him. During the depression of the late 1890s, despite all the problems in his struggles within the company-- Henry as a major stockholder--made money.

Even when he was temporarily tossed off the Quaker board by Schumacher and had to battle to regain his company, God still blessed him financially. In fact, it seemed that Henry amassed enormous wealth without even trying.

A case in point occurred just after he and his partner started the Perfection Stove Company. They began to see huge sales right from the beginning but then God presented Henry with a most unusual and wonderful surprise.

A Cleveland society family had moved to New York when their son was 14 years old. That son's name was John D. Rockefeller and when he grew up, he began an oil refinery business that became the Standard Oil Company. But the methods for refining petroleum at the turn of the century were still quite crude. As a result, a significant portion of every barrel of raw petroleum was turned into "coal oil" in the process of refining it. This "coal oil", or kerosene, accumulated in huge lakes and lagoons, with virtually no market for it except the old-fashioned lamps. But now, many of these were being replaced by gas or electric lamps.

In 1901, Henry's partner in Perfection Stove Company, Francis Drury, was approached by Rockefeller with a suggestion. Drury then told Henry about the meeting the next day.

"Seems that Standard Oil has these huge pools of coal oil that nobody wants," he explained. "And when they heard about our kerosene stoves, they figured our stoves might create a market for their coal oil. The way he put it is something.

Imagine if those who buy our stoves would buy Standard kerosene. Because it's a cook stove, customers use it every day, every day of the year. Before long, those huge lakes of coal oil would be sold. "

Henry listened and nodded from time to time. Then he asked, "It would take a lot more stoves than we've sold so far to market that much coal oil. You're talking about sales far beyond our capability. Even selling night and day, we couldn't sell that many."

"Well, Henry," Frank said excitedly. "They figured that out for themselves. Rockefeller wants to know if *their* salesmen can help by selling our stoves to create more stove users. He says it'll help create a market for their coal oil, and we'll sell a lot more stoves."

"How do they think that will help?"

"That's what is so incredible!" Frank replied. "They have *three thousand salesmen*--and Rockefeller said if we agree, they'll put all three thousand to work right away selling Perfection Stoves!"

While their company had been doing quite well already, this venture with Standard Oil Company brought Henry and his partner immediate astronomical sales that neither had even dreamed of having, even in a lifetime.

To Henry, such results were because of God's intervention. These were blessings that He pushed over the transom, surprising everyone. Henry was quick to properly credit Him for such incredible blessings. He said time and again to his family and co-workers, "I can never get ahead of God in the matter of giving! He is always there ahead of me with great surprises." Henry took much of the fortune which he had amassed from the stove sales to fund church and missionary ventures.

The second aspect of his stewardship was the use of his *personal time*, including how he dealt with others and what he could do for their individual spiritual or material needs. In this regard, he often took as much time to talk with elevator operators, people from the assembly line, floor sweepers, and others on lower rungs of the corporate ladder as the time he spent with tycoons.

Harry also encouraged others to consider the importance of their time in the same context, and give themselves to those who need their time.

Because he now had more leisure time, he could spend more of it in that area that non-believers find strange--an enterprise that Henry called *trying to lead others to Christ.*

His personal appointment book was filled with luncheon meetings or office chats with other business men concerning spiritual matters. He also, of course, continued to witness his faith personally in the church auditorium on Sundays, much to the chagrin of social snobs and the minister. But few had the courage to stop the millionaire from talking to anyone and everyone about the Lord.

Much of his other personal time went toward other church work, hosting Bible studies, and other involvements that were evangelistic in nature. Henry had a strong concern that others get the chance to meet Jesus Christ in the same way that he and Susan had.

The third aspect of his personal stewardship was his time as it related to the context of his influence and involvement--in *social action.* Because of his position as a powerful person in big business, Henry had a currency of another sort. He could bring about change, motivate people to action and see that things that might help society get implemented. God had blessed him with unusual wisdom, a quality he had used with determination. Others were quick to dispense their own pronouncements when decisions were required. Yet, Henry's style was more personal and deliberate. He would let people talk while he'd listen attentively. After a time of discussion and consideration, people usually then asked for *his* suggestions--and he gave them. Never at a loss in such situations where a decision was required, Henry not only had an answer to give--it was almost always the best solution being considered: *Take your time . . . find God's will.*

Once he understood and practiced this three-fold concept of stewardship, Henry felt it was divinely inspired. *Even my time was bought and paid for by my Savior,* he explained to his Bible class one day.

Chapter Twelve

Henry did not have to wait long once he had given God permission to make use of his time in social action opportunities. As Henry and Susan prayed, God seemed to speak to them about some very specific concerns. Within the shadow of their Rush Street residence, they saw growing evidence of vice and crime. In Cleveland, they'd often go off to church or visit another family and not even bother to lock their doors. Nor was there much in the way of crime and vice in their Ohio community.

But in Chicago at the turn of the century, thousands of young men and women had come to the city to find employment from towns in Wisconsin, Illinois and Indiana. However, during the depression of the late 1890s, jobs were scarce. Many of them were homeless and had no money. Young women, facing poverty and hunger, were easy prey for those who recruited them into prostitution. By 1900, this vice was so institutionalized that nearly everyone in Chicago knew about it.

The real beneficiaries of prostitution were a loose network of crooked politicians and policemen, saloon keepers, cab drivers, hotel bellhops, madams, bail bondsmen, lawyers, loan sharks and various others out to "help" the girls earn a living. The biggest losers, of course, were the young women themselves. They had to give commissions and kick-backs to several layers of "protectors" who helped them merchandise their bodies and souls.

Even in 1900 dollars, prostitution in Chicago was a million-dollar-a-month business. The mayor and other politicians seemed to wink at it and actually did little to clean it up or try to eliminate it. "After all," they reasoned, "we've always had prostitution and always will. Let's just try to keep it under control. We'll set aside a 'red light' district and leave it alone." This was the last straw as far as Henry was concerned. He began to protest the vice in Chicago by making it an issue in his church. But this was not effective.

Soon the houses of prostitution were not the only attractions in the red light district. Not far from the Cook County Building, storefront shops went up offering live, incredibly stark sex shows. Out of town salesmen frequented them and before long, the locals began to come. Then, even high school boys were let inside by the sidewalk hawkers.

Eventually, the sex shops, gin mills, "date houses", sleazy joints and houses of prostitution expanded and muscled their way into the more respectable business sectors of Chicago. Many of them were shamelessly guarded by crooked cops and sheltered by politicians who bought and sold protection. Finally, no longer contained by the established red light district, vice seemed to be everywhere. Still no one protested.

The church seemed ineffectual to deal with such an industry. Henry decided to take the matter to a few other civic minded industrialists. Dr. Clifford Barnes was a well-known social activist. Henry talked to him about this terrible blight in the midst of Chicago's Loop.

These two men then called on three others who agreed to meet with them. Henry asked civic-minded Julius Rosenwald, industrialist Harold Swift and *Chicago Tribune* publisher, Medill McCormick agreed to organize.

This *Committee of Five*, as they were to be known, had the ability to get the attention of the city. They said to Chicago's vice lords, *Enough is enough!* And finally, their protests were being heard. The *Committee of Five* decided to again establish virtue in the city and fight the underworld of vice and crime.

Warfare against the underworld was not to be taken lightly, however. The crooks, thieves and hookers had more manpower and money than did the crusaders. They played down their evils only when it was in the best interests of their business to do so. They closed down something only if it took the public's attention away from a more lucrative vice that they *didn't* close down.

The red light district did not go away. So the *Committee of Five* stepped up its efforts. They pressured the State's Attorney to investigate and prosecute vice with real vigor and honest effort. The public finally began to protest as well. As Henry and the other four men continued to work to shut down prostitution and crime, other civic leaders were recruited to help. The committee was renamed *Committee of Fifteen*, with a board of directors of some 50 other civic leaders. With this added clout, they pressured the mayor and prosecutors to "do something about the vice problems".

And it worked. First, the *Committee of Fifteen* pushed through enactment of a federal law called the Mann Act, which made it a crime to transport young women across state lines for immoral purposes. Next, they got the Illinois legislature to pass a law against pandering.

One of the members of the *Committee of Fifteen*, Medill McCormick, so pressured the mayor through coverage in his *Chicago Tribune* that the mayor was forced to act. Grudgingly, he shut down some of the most notorious prostitution houses in the red light district.

When the State's Attorney seemed to be dragging his feet, the *Tribune* also took him to task. The next day, 135 warrants were served to shut down more houses of prostitution.

The *Committee of Fifteen* next pressured local government to pass an Injunction and Abatement Law that would effectively wipe out the entire seedy business. Some 500 places were investigated and most of them shut down by vice cops. All in all, the pressure was kept up by Henry and the other civic minded leaders for some twenty years, as long as Henry served on the *Committee of Fifteen.*

Henry also became a charter member of the Chicago Crime Commission which was created to improve the city's police force and help drive out crime and underworld influences. This was in the era that mobster Al Capone was starting to make a name for himself.

Through the efforts of the *Committee of Fifteen* and the Chicago Crime Commission, Henry used his stewardship of time, money and wisdom for unique and positive change. But instead of being content with simply shutting down a sinful establishment or driving loan sharks out of town, Henry felt something had to go into the vacuum that such eviction created. Otherwise, he reasoned, someone else will come along and start up all over again--something he'd already witnessed many times.

It was a good feeling to have a law enacted or a reform sponsored that was designed to help the people. But even more satisfying to Henry was when a sector of the business community met needs represented by the original problem. It wasn't enough to eliminate loan sharks. They existed because the poor or less advantaged had to borrow money and previously had nowhere else to turn. So when savings banks for the poor and working classes were formed just to meet this need, Henry had a deep sense of personal satisfaction.

One man can make a difference, as D. L. Moody had once preached to him.

Henry's influence on the lives of many in business had not gone unnoticed. His friend, Dr. Newell, had told him about serious problems at Moody Bible Institute. The great evangelist had just died and the school seemed about to suffer the same consequences. MBI Board members Dr. Will Norton and Dr. James Gray met with Henry and asked for his advice.

Dr. Gray had been hand-picked by D. L. Moody to come to MBI and lecture to the students and faculty. A drift toward doctrinal extremes had worried Moody; he wanted someone who knew both the Bible and sound doctrine to come and set his students and faculty on the right path. Dr. Gray had just begun that assignment, which would affiliate him with the school for the rest of his life. These men were committed to saving the spiritual life of the school.

When he had first heard about Moody's school from his friend, William Newell, Henry was much impressed by the quality of men the famous evangelist had drawn around him. They were capable Bible scholars and effective teachers. The central theme of the school was a devotion to the Bible and its inerrancy. Its mission was to train pastors, missionaries and Christian workers.

Yet, the school had nothing--no real assets or practical facilities, no respect, no plans for the future. Nothing.

Dr. Newell called his friend Henry Crowell to come and look into the problem and hopefully help MBI. He introduced Henry to Dr. James M. Gray, president of the school, who sat across from Henry in Moody's old room at the Institute. As the two sat on opposite sides of the table, each tried to assess the other.

Dr. Gray talked and Henry listened. Then they prayed. This was the way they assessed each other's heart. From this quiet and unassuming beginning, an alliance was formed. Dr. Gray would see to the educational and spiritual aspect of the Institute. Henry Crowell would look to the business side.

As Henry listened to its leaders, he was impressed that they were godly men, but recognized that they knew virtually nothing about how to run an organization. As a result, MBI was dying, mostly because of limited funding and lack of a business plan. While he was alive, Moody could go to church and business leaders and ask for money for his school. But now he was gone. There was no one else on the staff or faculty who had the gift for stepping into Moody's shoes and getting the funds for keeping the school alive.

Henry gave them the unvarnished truth. "D. L. Moody knew how to raise money from his friends. But he's gone now, and there are no more friends of Moody to give the kind of money it takes to run this business."

Dr. Gray arched his eyebrow at Henry's candor and use of the word *business*. To Henry, this *was* a business. It needed capital to pay the costs of providing a service--training young ministers and missionaries for God's service. Without taking anything from the men who came to teach the Bible, it was acutely obvious to Henry that none of them really understood the business of running such an organization, or even if they could read a typical financial statement of assets, liabilities, capital, income and expenses.

Under Crowell, Moody Bible Institute was built on business principles and a foundation of productivity and performance. The MBI Executive Committee met on Tuesdays, nearly every week. So, one day every week, for 40 years, Henry gave himself to Moody. He put the school on a sound financial basis. Sometimes that meant putting his own money on the line. He did so quietly, without fanfare and without attaching strings to his gifts.

Henry showed the school how to plan as if it were a business. For buildings, he saw to it that they went only as far into construction as they had funding for. Dormitories and offices were done in stages, as funds came in. An administration building took years to complete, but when the building was dedicated, there was no mortgage, and only $50,000 left to pay.

Henry had provided about half the cost of the newly constructed Moody administration building, but few knew that. The new president of MBI, Dr. Will Houghton, wanted to name the building in Henry's honor, and came to his Quaker Oats office to discuss it.

"Henry, we're just about ready to complete the new building. Some of the faculty and trustees were talking, and we have unanimous agreement. We want the stonecutters to put *Crowell Hall* above the entrance arch. What do you say?" he asked.

Henry did not answer right away. His mind went back to that church meeting in Ohio where he heard D. L. Moody speak on how one man can make a difference. And how he had asked God to allow him to make money for His causes. Then Henry recalled the latter half of his agreement: . . . *and I'll keep my name out of it. It'll be for Your glory!*

The answer was clear. "No, Dr. Houghton. I can't let you do that. I told God I'd keep my name out of it. And I will. Find another name for it." This was his final word on the matter.

Despite his generous giving, however, Henry's goal was to find others to help Moody get on its financial feet. It could never depend on a single person for funding; what MBI needed was a number of friends who would be reliable in their support. Henry Crowell showed the school's leaders how to find such friends and keep them. He created an Annuity Plan that not only provided financial stability for the school and funded the training of young men and women for Christian work, it gave income for the annuitants. As in so many of his business ideas, Henry had created a "win-win" situation.

In the years of his leadership, MBI became a highly respected Chicago institution and provided world-wide accomplishments for the kingdom of Christ. Throughout its history, MBI has acknowledged the input and stewardship of Henry Parsons Crowell as strategic to its success and phenomenal growth.

It was Henry who pointed Moody Bible Institute toward its involvement in modern communications. His own experience in advertising and marketing taught him that these tools can be effective in reaching men and women for Christ. He helped MBI start a viable book publishing enterprise--from the old Moody Colportage Association he created Moody Press which took some of his marketing ideas to sell books. Next, he started a monthly magazine and pioneered in brand new fields of technology. He got the Institute to lead the way in one of these newer technologies--*radio.*

A few years earlier, when radio was *really* an infant, Henry had used it to test market a Quaker promotion. He offered a radio crystal set (which used a Quaker oatmeal box replica as the tuning coil). The kit came with all the components for $1.00 plus a box top--and for $5.00 plus a box top, you'd get the kit and a set of earphones.

The company was swamped with orders--some 250,000 of these radio kits were sold instantly and even more were sold when the offer was repeated two years later. By then, Henry advertised heavily on radio. Many had scoffed that no one was listening, let alone would respond. But people *were* listening, and they did respond. Sales of Quaker breakfast foods skyrocketed. Radio was a powerful new way to reach vast audiences.

Henry saw the fantastic potential of spreading the gospel with this mysterious new medium and he pushed MBI to be at the cutting edge of those using this amazing communications tool. When he first introduced the idea of using radio, there were only a handful of radio broadcasting stations in the entire country and just three million radios, mostly crystal sets. The number of sets was increasing daily and Henry Crowell wanted Moody to be the first to use the exciting new medium of radio for Christian purposes.

WMBI was one of the first radio stations in the country and was state of the art, with a high-powered transmitter, tower, studios and staff that was totally committed to the cause of Christ. At the dedication ceremonies, a statement said, in part,

The Cereal Tycoon

We dedicate this broadcasting station tonight . . . as a witness that the Church is the body of which Christ is the Head, and that its mission is to carry the gospel of salvation to all men and to every nation under heaven, for which purpose it is that the young men and women in the Institute are being trained.

To build and operate a high-powered radio broadcasting station in the early days of the 20th Century was audacious. It would be as revolutionary as some Christian organization today getting into a new technology still in its infancy--such as one of today's satellite digital interactive video and computer networks. Henry Crowell saw value in radio--and somehow he saw a future giving this technology a multiplied effectiveness in spreading the gospel not just in Chicago but worldwide.

*   *   *   *

Henry Crowell had learned early in life to expect change. He easily adapted to it and many times even embraced it. There seemed to be no challenge too big or impossible. When told that Americans only ate pancakes during cold weather, and that this food was perceived as only a winter tradition, Henry scoffed. "We'll just have to change that habit," he smiled. "Why shouldn't people be able to eat pancakes anytime they want?"

So, with advertising, merchandising and creating market demand, he sold America on the idea that his Aunt Jemima Pancake Mix was good all year round. This willingness to confront traditional thought was something Henry used to advantage in the Christian arena as well. Already he had people wondering about Moody's ventures into radio. "Radio!? Humphh!" Some clucked, "It's wrong. Radio comes over the airwaves, and after all, the devil is the 'prince of the power of the air' and it says so right in the Bible!"

But Henry's ideas prevailed. There were other Christian projects to which he devoted his time. At the time he was working with the *Committee of Fifteen* in trying to clean up Chicago, he also worked to give Christianity a highly visible presence in the city, heading the Layman's Evangelistic Council during these years and organizing some of Chicago's most historic evangelistic crusades.

In 1907, for a month, tent meetings were held near Moody featuring the dynamic preacher, R. A. Torrey. Two years later, Henry urged the committee to have faith that Gipsy Smith would fill the 6,000 seat Seventh Regular Armory. These meetings also lasted a month and brought what was described as a city-wide moral and spiritual revival.

Then, in 1911, Henry brought in the team of Chapman and Alexander campaigning in two locations for two weeks each. These also brought salvation and spiritual healing to the city of Chicago.

The most dramatic and historic event by far, however, was the appearance a few years later by a former White Stockings baseball player. William Ashley Sunday had been soundly converted at the Pacific Garden Mission on South State Street in Chicago several years earlier. Now, "Billy" Sunday was back in Chicago, ready to battle the devil!

As an advertising and marketing genius, Henry already knew how to mobilize the press and he invited them to cover the Billy Sunday Crusade. Of course, the Chicago papers had a heyday with the pulpit gymnastics and colloquial manner of the animated evangelist. But excerpts of his sermons were also carried by the newspapers. The publicity helped draw larger crowds for the closing days of the crusade.

Henry never sought the spotlight when it came to the stewardship of his time. He gave many months every year to his church. A new pastor was more tolerant, even appreciative of his efforts to confront people in the church auditorium about their spiritual needs. Henry also taught a Bible class for business leaders and students. No church assignment was too large or too small.

By now, Henry had been elected Chairman of the Board at Quaker Oats. He left it to others to run the day to day operations, and gave more of his time to the causes he held dear. The three-fold stewardship credo--money, time for personal involvement in church causes, and time devoted to effecting social change--guided his actions in giving back to God what the Lord had so graciously given to him.

Chapter Thirteen

God seemed to have truly blessed the efforts of Henry Crowell and Robert Stuart when they returned to leadership at Quaker Oats, after the ouster of Ferdinand Schumacher. There was unparalleled growth of sales and net operating profit. In 1911 the treasurer told common stock shareholders that they had earned nearly 25% return on their investment, unheard of during a time of serious recession as the country was currently experiencing.

The same thing happened the next year, and the next. By sound management and using biblical values to guide his decisions, Henry made Quaker Oats the ideal investment for its shareholders. The company prospered even in bad times, and was often able to take advantage of these bad times to further their leadership position.

During 1911, the same year the company did so well, another company ran into serious trouble. The Great Western Cereal Company had been formed to specifically challenge and destroy Quaker Oats. For years the company had been cash short and losing money. As a last ditch effort to recover, they spent huge sums on advertising, but without the Crowell touch and effectiveness. Sales did not happen and all their money was spent and the Great Western Cereal Company was unable to continue. Bankrupt and hat in hand, it offered its assets to Quaker for $1 million plus the value of its grain inventory.

If Henry didn't buy the company, their plants would be shut down, forcing thousands of people out of work and losing millions of dollars for its shareholders. So Quaker Oats agreed to buy the bankrupt company.

After the sale, government regulators stepped in, accusing Quaker of anti-trust violations. The U. S. Attorney General said that Quaker was trying to swallow up its competition and become a cereal monopoly. "Not only that", he said, "I believe that Quaker and Great Western have acted in collusion to transfer the assets of the bankrupt company at greatly reduced prices to defraud the stockholders." He also accused Quaker and Great Western of price fixing.

Other accusations flew back and forth, and Quaker found itself in the midst of a serious federal prosecution. Henry knew each company had acted in good faith and along proper guidelines. As to Quaker monopolizing the cereal trade, Henry smiled ironically. There were 108 different brand names of corn flakes alone! Yet, proving their innocence to an antagonistic Attorney General was going to be difficult.

At a lengthy and costly trial, the case went before a panel of three federal judges. Most of the officers of Great Western appeared as government witnesses in an attempt to bolster the government's claim of price fixing. But the two key officers of the company told the truth on the witness stand. The cause of going bankrupt, they admitted, was the huge sums of money they spent on advertising, trying to compete with Quaker's highly successful ads. The result, however, was absolute failure. Their ads didn't work.

Quaker refuted the claim that they'd taken advantage of Great Western and bilked its shareholders by paying a low price for its assets. Under oath, the Great Western officers admitted that if Quaker had not come forward with $1 million, the stockholders would have received *nothing* for their company because it would have declared bankruptcy.

One of the federal judges was not convinced. He accused Quaker of acting to kill off competition. Henry winced. If the other two judges felt the same way, the case was lost.

As the other judges rendered their verdicts, they were in agreement with each other--but *not* with the dissenting judge. They held for Quaker in a majority decision, agreeing that Quaker had acted in a proper manner and that the bankruptcy of its competitor contributed to *its own* downfall; that Quaker was *not guilty of anti-trust violations*. The case collapsed and the government's charges were dismissed.

The heavy costs of fighting the anti-trust suit probably put a dent in the Quaker profit margins over those years, but the overall financial picture continued to increase.

World War I was even a time of profitability. Grain prices, as a result of the war and severe crop failures, were at the highest prices in 50 years. Other cereal businesses used the war as a reason to raise prices. It would have been easy to gouge the public or the government for the military orders needed for troops overseas.

But Quaker Oats issued a public statement that the company would not take advantage of the war and profit from the shortages. Even so, sales doubled from the previous highs and validated their moral stand.

In creating new ways to merchandise cereal and other food products, Henry Crowell also made it possible for other pioneers to flourish. By establishing distribution methods which had never been done before, he opened the door for grocery chains to replace the inefficient general stores. It wasn't long before A & P Stores expanded to 500 stores, and was soon opening a new store every three days. Alpha Beta, starting in California, launched an expansion nearly as extensive. This was followed by Ward's Grocertia on the East Coast and the Humpty Dumpty chain in California.

Railroad freight charges dropped from the $1.22 per ton/mile in 1883 to just 75 cents by 1900. There were a quarter million miles of train tracks, but in addition, there were 190,000 miles of paved roads by 1916, compared with *just 200 miles* just 16 years earlier!

Yet, the times were apocalyptic. Clergymen preached about this era as the "end times" referred to in the Bible. In addition, global war in Europe killed some 10 million and blinded, maimed or otherwise crippled another 20 million. The worst plague pandemic in 500 years killed 21 million people, mostly in the war zones and poorer countries.

In America, the people suffered with food shortages, and paid for the war with terrifically high taxes. Rationing curbed distribution of many foods and other materials. Famine and drought in Europe, especially in Russia, killed millions more by the time of the Armistice on November 11, 1918.

After the war, 20,000 American businesses failed and 3.5 million workers lost their jobs. In Germany, inflation was rampant, with the exchange rate by 1922 exploding to and incredible 4.2 million marks to the U. S. dollar. German farmers fared best. They bartered batches of eggs, milk, butter or bread for pianos, sewing machines and even Rembrandt paintings or Persian rugs.

But probably the worst experience for Henry during the first part of the century was the declining health of his wife, Susan. Some years earlier, her health had deteriorated to the point where the couple began to look for a place with a more friendly climate than the fierce winters of Chicago. They prayed about where they might move for the winter season, looking first at Florida, then settling on Georgia.

In 1909, they discovered the former residence of a former governor, Charles Jones Jenkins, located just outside

Augusta, and renovated it with additions, a beautiful garden, walks, and a vast area of azaleas and other shrubs and trees.

Inside, there were a number of rooms, including a library with a vast collection of books, parlors for reading and conversations by the fireplace, dining rooms for entertaining and large verandas facing the flowering gardens and shrubs.

Susan felt immediately at home here, as did Henry, and they named the place *Green Court*. To the couple, it was like heaven. Their winter home was a quiet retreat from the terrible things going on in the world, and from the stresses of business. Henry and Susan took long, lingering walks through the garden, prayed together on the veranda, and opened their home in Augusta to the community.

Their son, Henry Coleman Crowell, had grown up in Chicago and had gone away to study at Yale. In July, 1919, he came to *Green Court* to announce his engagement to Miss Lucy Perry Kimball. After the initial excitement of the engagement party died down, Henry took Lucy for a walk in the garden.

"Tell me, Lucy," he smiled, "how you two met, and all the details leading up to your decision to marry."

The young woman, shy at first, did as she was asked and told the older man beside her how she had met and fell in love with his son. Henry reached out and held her hands and smiled once more. "Susan and I prayed for Coleman," he told Lucy. "We prayed every step of the way, even for God to choose the woman he was to marry some day, and I just wanted to see how the Lord answered our prayer."

In the fall, Coleman went back to Yale to finish up his final year of university studies. They were married the following year in Evanston.

Not long after that Susan was conducting Bible studies in her living room, and Henry was leading a men's Bible class. Their winter residence had become, as had their Chicago home, a place for men and women to find Christ and grow spiritually. From this origin, others were invited to teach and speak.

Missionaries and Christian speakers taught classes whenever the Crowells weren't in residence.

The churches surrounding the area in Augusta were great beneficiaries of this godly presence in *Green Court*. It was here that many society couples found Christ.

A young woman named Katherine talked about her experience. "I was a cigarette smoking, cocktail drinking, small town rich girl. My father, an Augusta attorney, was educated abroad; he was a brilliant agnostic." she said. "He and mother never went to church."

Katherine decided by age 17 that there was no God. But for seven years, some who knew her prayed for her at the *Green Court* chapel sessions. Finally, a friend "dragged" her to a Bible class. Mrs. George Rounds was the teacher and Katherine was put off by the "stodgy" retired missionary.

"When I laid eyes on Mrs. Rounds--that did it!" Katherine recalled. "What could that old thing do for me? Why--she looks mildewed!" But one day, her heart melted and she gave herself wholeheartedly to Christ.

This godly use of their home in Augusta continued for 13 years. Then, Susan's health took a turn for the worse, even in the warmer climate. On a warm June day in 1922, a year after Coleman and Lucy were married, Susan died.

Henry and Susan had been married 34 years and she left Henry behind, lonely and with his heart broken at the loss of his sweetheart. Yet there was no doubting that God had blessed Henry Crowell, through good times and bad.

Chapter Fourteen

Following the death of his wife, Susan, Henry, at 67, continued to busy himself in what he called "the Lord's work". Back in Chicago, he took the train to the office every day and once or more during the week, walked the mile or so distance from his offices in the Board of Trade Building to Moody Bible Institute on North LaSalle Street. His son, Coleman, did not follow in his father's footsteps and go to work for Quaker Oats. Instead, he felt called to Moody where he could put his talents to use in business adminstration there. He was so good at it that Coleman quickly became the C.E.O. of the Institute.

When Henry wasn't busy at either Quaker Oats or Moody, he was usually involved with the *Committee of Fifteen* and their attempts to curb vice and crime in Chicago. This was during the Prohibition era, and Al Capone had wrestled control of the various mob factions in the city and now ruled with a violent hand.

The gang lord's illicit businesses--bootleg liquor, prostitution, loan sharking, extortion, pornography and drugs were earning the mob more than *$4 billion* a year--even in the currency values of the Twenties. Al Capone himself was reported to be earning $105 million a year--$35 million more than Henry Ford, considered to be America's most productive industrialist.

Capone's gang earned much of its revenues from the illicit liquor trade. The whiskey distilleries had been closed by the government at the start of Prohibition and all alcoholic beverages were banned. Capone ran illegal breweries and distilleries, but the drinks took their toll. Thousands of Americans were killed or blinded by bad liquor, but the crime associated with the bootleg and other Capone businesses flourished.

On Valentine's Day in 1929, gang warfare had reached its peak when seven members of a rival gang were executed in a North Clark Street garage. Police suspected that Al Capone's gang was behind the "massacre" but those seven deaths were only a small fraction of the 498 murders in the city that year.

Later, in October, the city of Chicago, along with the rest of the world, had much more to worry about when the stock market crashed and brought on the Great Depression. Overnight $30 billion in capital was wiped out. There was an epidemic of suicides among stock speculators. Thousands of businesses failed in the months following.

Not everything in the Twenties was gloomy, however. Despite crime and financial instability, Americans had been moving up the ladder of prosperity. Model T autos sold as fast as Ford could make them and the price was half that paid only a few years earlier. Americans were becoming a mobile society.

Communications companies expanded the business and social lives of Americans. NBC Radio had 31 radio affiliates, while newcomer CBS started up with 22 affiliates. Now, even cars were being sold with Motorola radios. Over 20 million Americans had telephones; there was even a new Transatlantic phone service connecting America with Britain and the rest of Europe at an astronomical cost of $75 for three minutes of conversation.

Despite the Depression, a fledgling airline industry was launched, with United, TWA, American Airlines, Pan Am and Braniff making flights to key cities in somewhat irregular service.

The economy collapsed during the Thirties, though. American unemployment was 4 million in 1930, doubled to 8 million a year later, doubled again during the next six months and again by the end of 1931, when 34 million were out of work and one in four Americans had no job.

Through the Depression, God had continued to bless Henry Crowell and he did not suffer financially. However, he saw the need to conserve his financial resources from eroding. If he didn't, it would limit his many stewardship opportunities. Henry also had interests beyond his role as benefactor in Christian institutions. So, it was a time not just of conserving his wealth, but of protecting it from those who were captured by growing unbelief and the trends toward liberal, unbiblical doctrines in many of the traditional mainstream denominations and organizations.

When his own denomination began to drift away from core beliefs and doctrines, Henry became concerned. Ironically, money and assets provided by devoted and doctrinally sound people were being subverted by those who had no use for their faith or beliefs. Henry knew such "piracy" would never be tolerated in his world, the business world. When he looked into the process called *modernism*, Henry saw that it nearly always began at the religious colleges and universities.

Teachers were hired for their scholarship, and no mention was made of their belief structure. And while none of these irreligious professors would really describe himself as an atheist, the results were nonetheless the same. Young people, reared in evangelical, orthodox homes and churches, went away to school only to have their faith ravaged by those who tore down the Bible and its doctrines, referred to as mere myths and traditions.

Evolutionary thought, denying such essential doctrines as the virgin birth, atonement, deity of Christ, matters relating to the integrity of the Bible and other Christian cardinal tenets became the issues of the modernists. Henry began to see how effectively these views were in destroying faith and undermining Christian values.

The mainstream churches of the day were not at all like the parish of Dr. Hawks, where Henry had met his Savior as a ten-year-old boy in the minister's study. Today's churches were more and more like the apostasy Dr. Newell had described nearly half a century before in the Bible classes in their Rush Street home.

Henry realized that attacks on Christian faith led to the same place--the loss of successive generations of believers. He knew the value and validity of his faith and beliefs and how these had been the basis for his entire life of business and Christian enterprises. Now, he understood, it was not enough that believers put godly men and women into positions of leadership. These godly people must also surround themselves with others who share their beliefs. If someone is hired who is not of faith, he has the opportunity to bring down all the work which others have erected before him.

Henry was convinced that all leaders and workers in a Christian organization must be intolerant of unbelievers in positions of real authority because that unbelief eventually undermines the faith of those who believe in God and the Bible.

As he reflected over these events, Henry shuddered. *It might happen,* he thought, *that after I am gone, unbelievers might come in as trustees and use the assets of my estate against the gospel and everything that I believe in!*

If Henry understood anything, it was how fickle courts can be in interpreting agreements and contracts. If he left money in his will for a denomination, or a school, or any organization for that matter, how could he know for certainty that in 10 years, even 50 years from now, that organization would still be faithful to God and essential Christian tenets.

He must find some way to keep his fortune intact after his death so that it will continue to work for Christ's causes and not be appropriated by the modernists or other disclaimers of faith. He wrote down a few notes and decided to talk to his lawyer about such a plan.

"What this sounds like to me," remarked his attorney, Frank Loesch, "is a trust. That's probably the way to go."

"Well, Frank," said Henry, "you've heard my side of it. I want my assets to go to God's work, but I want to be protected from the wiles of the devil and those who may come along later to lead believers astray. I don't want my money doing that kind of work after I'm gone!"

Loesch was a long time friend and confidant who had a great reputation in his ability to draw up estate documents. "Tell me what you want," he asked Henry.

"Well, first of all, I'd like to leave the bulk of my personal fortune in such a way as to protect it for years to come from theft."

"Theft?"

"I don't want it stolen by trustees or those who do not share my faith and values."

"Then we should create a trust so its benefits can be handled *ad vitam aut culpam*," the attorney replied. "But of course, insuring that *quamdiu se beni gesserit*."

"English, please," Henry asked.

Frank Loesch smiled. "It means, basically, *'for life, without fault'* that is, *'so long as he behaves well'*."

He explained the structure to Henry. "First, there are five *secret* trustees. By keeping them anonymous, they won't be pressured by outside influences. These trustees must affirm, in writing, every year that they are in agreement with the terms and standards of the trust. You can set up the standards in the trust itself to measure your trustees. They have to affirm belief in these tenets or resign. And if any one trustee does not measure up, the other four can replace him! The trustees are self-perpetuating, secretly appointing others of like mind to fill any vacancies."

Henry smiled and nodded in agreement. The attorney continued, "Any contributions given are given individually, and nothing is endowed in perpetuity, so every gift can be reviewed to make sure the beneficiary lives up to your standards of faith as well. And that's good on his part, too. He can never take it for granted that any appropriation made to his organization is permanent. That way, if any organization drifts toward modernism, the trustees can cut it off. No more money!"

"Sounds good to me," said Henry. He named this agreement *The Henry Parsons Crowell and Susan Coleman Crowell Trust*. Although Susan had died many years earlier, he said that the trust was as much hers as his and he wanted it to reflect her wishes as well his own.

*　　　*　　　*　　　*

During his lifetime, Henry had made money in ways that staggered the imagination. Friends joked that he could make money even in failure.

Just before WWI Henry was approached by a friend in Denver to whom he had loaned money to go into the cattle business. However, the man was not successful and Henry had to take back the cattle herd and property used as collateral for the money he had loaned.

Recalling with fond memories his earlier exploits with the Percheron horse ranch in North Dakota, Henry decided to take over the Wyoming Hereford Ranch and try to make it successful. He added more range land to the property, giving it a total of *55,000 acres*, on land a mile high, just east of Cheyenne. It was more like an empire than a cattle ranch. Before long, Henry had purchased several thousand cattle, including 50 breeding bulls to start the herd.

To the amazement of all in the business, Henry did not hire an experienced ranch hand to manage the business. Instead, he hired a recent University of Michigan graduate, Robert Lazear, son of his friend, George.

When asked why he'd hire a "greenhorn" to run the ranch, Henry replied, "The problem was, to find a leader. There were a lot of men out there who had lots of opinions and traditions. But they couldn't think of new ways to do things. They seemed afraid of new methods and ideas. Bob, on the other hand, was fresh out of school and eager to try new things. He was trained as an engineer, strong, a nature lover, and most important--a Christian."

Whenever he could, Henry hired Christians, saying, "Man for man, a Christian will always go further." His judgment was proven correct in the case of Bob Lazear who was unfazed by past ways of doing the job, finding new ways of accomplishing "impossible" things. After 18 successful years, the ranch earned international acclaim for its breeding work and Henry was honored for his contributions to that area of scientific research.

Thus, even a "failed" Hereford ranch business, with the Crowell touch, became a money-maker. However, Susan's death some years earlier had impressed upon Henry a vision of his own mortality. He knew that his time on earth was limited, so Henry decided to find a way to let the Wyoming Hereford Ranch continue after his death.

He formed a trust, similar to the one he had created for his personal wealth, and put the assets and income from the Wyoming Hereford Ranch into it in order to perpetuate its activities, assuring Bob Lazear that he'd be cared for during his employment and retirement years that followed.

Here was another way that the works of Henry Crowell could follow him, could continue in his absence. But for the time being, his health was still robust and his life busy.

By way of contrast, though, the country's health was not as good. America was still the middle of the Depression, and financial ruin was rampant. Already more than 1,600 banks had closed, along with 20,000 businesses. Even major cities failed--such as Detroit, which defaulted on $400 million in bond debt because of the bank closings. Other major cities followed suit. The number of suicides was past 21,000 and counting. Nearly a million Americans, no longer able to feed themselves, moved back to the farms to live off the land. Another million farm families had to go on relief to keep from starving.

As if the financial woes were not enough, the country was plagued by huge dust storms that *destroyed between 100 and 300 million acres* of croplands. Dust Bowl farmers, eager to cash in on high grain prices during WWI a dozen years earlier had plowed the virgin lands without regard for conservation. When the great winds came, they blew away the rich topsoil forever. Drought continued for several successive years, followed by diseases that killed the grain.

Overseas, famine and apocalyptic diseases killed millions, and millions of others were tortured and killed by terrible despots like Josef Stalin in Russia.

Despite the terrible plagues of the Depression years, there were some bright spots. Prohibition ended in 1933. Of course, that meant that Americans could once again drink alcohol legally, and its abuse would cause continuing problems. But it also meant that the Capone gang and other mobsters would lose a great deal of their $4 billion-a-year industry of vice, crime and corruption.

With the reelection of Franklin D. Roosevelt, the fortunes of America began to change and Depression times turned better. Yet, other troubles were beginning in Europe as Hitler brought the world into another great war.

Henry's businesses continued to prosper during the war years. His Perfection Stove Company, which had already expanded into other lines--water heaters, space heaters and furnaces, was recruited by the government to make camp stoves for the troops. The company built other military needs, such as aircraft doors, windshields and heaters.

Stock in Quaker Oats continued to pay top dividends and earn more money to be used for God's causes. Henry continued as chairman of the board of Quaker Oats until 1942, when at age 85, he was elected chairman emeritus. Still, busy as ever, he walked the mile to Moody on Tuesdays, every day briskly walking the seven blocks (each way) to take the Northwestern train to or from his home in Winnetka.

There is little evidence of old age slowing him down. His daily agenda was full, with much time spent reviewing requests from worthy causes coming to the *Crowell Trust*.

But as he thought more about the issues of modernism still tearing at the fabric of evangelical faith, even in his own denomination, Henry was convinced that it was important for him to take a stand. After a lifetime in his own church denomination, Henry decided to write to his pastor and resign from both the church and denomination.

In his letter, Henry cited certain recent unbiblical decisions of the denomination, its election of a man whom he believed lacked the "character, ability and fitness in meeting the problems that will have to be continued while the Assembly is in session." Then he questioned how the leadership, comprised of so many clear minds and hearts that valued the Bible and its essential truths, could recognize and elect a modernist of many years' standing.

"I have protested against modernism before and have done many things that I have hoped might check it, but the present issue and its apparent popularity indicate that the trend is now stronger than ever," Henry wrote. He added, "There is one more protest that I can make and as I have been led to it through prayer, communion, and fellowship with the Lord Jesus Christ, I make it known to you. I desire to sever all relationships that I have with the denomination and hereby resign from membership in the church. I also hereby retire from the office of Elder in the church."

Henry concluded his letter, "Something should be done at once to stop this drift toward modernism and I have thought of nothing better than for me to withdraw from the church as a definite forceful protest against changing standards and the weakening of the church's loyalty and devotion to Jesus Christ. I can serve the Lord elsewhere with a clear conscience, warm heart, and responsive love that will keep me ever in close union and fellowship with my Savior who loves me and gave Himself for my salvation and that of all who come to Him by faith."

However, the protest had little effect. His pastor and denominational leaders kept Henry's letter from being made public. Still, Henry discovered that those in leadership of evangelical schools and denominations welcomed his views.

Henry Parsons Crowell, in 1943, nearly 90 and still going to the office every day, seemed a paradox. His body, indeed, had the look of an old man. But his mind was almost youthful in its grasp of events and ideas.

For nearly 70 years, since he was 19, Henry had been active in business--successfully so. In his leadership role in the various companies he'd started, he was strict, confident, authoritative. Some might even say stubborn. Yet, his was a stubbornness borne out of the desire to do right. There would be no compromise in essential things. In business, his associates knew he would be unyielding in matters of ethics and morality, in the quality of his products or services, or in the principles of financial honesty and fairness. In matters of personal piety, those who knew him were impressed with his conviction to serve God faithfully, to give God his time and money, and to work diligently for His causes.

He had habits of personal prayer and devotion that would shame most ministers. These habits were as important to him as eating or breathing. Every morning, he would read while traveling on the train from Winnetka to the Loop in Chicago. Other commuters were engrossed in the *Tribune* or *Sun-Times*, but Henry Crowell would quietly and without fanfare take out his small *New Testament* from an inside pocket and begin to read. It was well worn and marked with notes in the margins, and while others devoured the latest sports scores, Mr. Crowell worshipped his Lord.

In such seriousness, strangers who met him for the first time might mistake this man of faith and principle to be austere, cold and perhaps even a stern taskmaster. But not those who got to know him. Under the outward, seemingly severe exterior, was a man whose heart was warm with Christian love and sincere natural affection.

True, he could be impatient with sloppy, careless work, or with liars and cheats. Also, in religious circles, many clergymen or ecclesiastical leaders felt the heat of his complaints if they drifted away from evangelical faith or the Bible.

He was not an eccentric rich old man who was simply tolerated in circles because of his wealth or contributions. He was valued, even at 89, for his wisdom, insight and valuable contributions to decision making.

These were the lessons he had learned as a boy. His first role model was his father, who taught him family values and stewardship. Then, his boyhood pastor who led him to Christ and pointed the way, the "narrow" way, of the cross. The other major role model of his youth was President Benjamin Mills, founder of his school, Greylock Institute, who taught the boy how to think and the disciplines of faith and work that established his character for life.

Now Henry was the role model. Letters in his files testified to his importance in literally thousands of lives.

Some samples include one written by a young pastor who was chastised for being too fervent in his sermons and advised to be more "cooperative" lest he be overlooked when the time came to be given a new pastorate. Should he give in to the modernist trends of his denomination, or continue to proclaim the Biblical truths as God reveals them to him? He answered his own question in a letter to Mr. Crowell:

Dear Sir,
Yesterday it came to my attention that you had done something that required real courage . . . due to conditions in your denomination, you severed your connections. . . . I am a young pastor and have admired you, expected the best of

you and have never been disappointed in you. . . . Again, you prove your real worth. . . . It was hard for you as a business man to take that step. But it proves that Christ is first in your life. . . . And He shall be first in mine!

A prominent business leader wrote:

Dear Mr. Crowell,
The first time I heard your name was about 25 years ago when I used to take my mother to Moody Bible Institute because she liked evangelism. . . . but I did not know much about you. . . . I have come to realize that you have had in mind all the time that if we are to preserve the influence of Christian religion in this country, as it was understood by pioneer Americans, then we must depend on religious evangelism rather than political evangelism. . . . You have had in mind religious evangelism; leading souls to Christ. And that is the only sort worth keeping. And the sort I have come to esteem through you!"

A well-known Chicago merchant wrote:

Dear Sir,
I saw you, when I was a young man, walking along Michigan Avenue. I was so attracted to you that I followed you, not once but several times. . . . You became to me a clear burning torch. . . . Mr. Crowell, your biography should be written and given to every young business man in America. I know others will be as blessed by your life as I have been.

And there were letters from students whose school tuition and lodging were paid by Mr. Crowell, missionaries who were helped with medical or living expenses, and from countless others to whom he had been an influence or benefactor.

A poor, blind woman regained her eyesight through an operation paid for by Mr. Crowell. She wrote:

Dear Mr. Crowell:
I hope very soon to come to the Fourth Church in order to get
a good look at you from a distance. Please pardon my joy at
the thought of it, for you know you helped me get my eyesight
back and how can I do otherwise than look at you with an
enthusiasm which is well nigh adoration?

These were his real treasures. To have wealth was only a
means that others kept score on life achievement. Henry
Crowell found contentment in things that had nothing to do
with material gain.

Chapter Fifteen

God had blessed Mr. Crowell in old age with a keen
mind and good health. As a rule, he walked every day to the
train, and once a week to his board meetings at Moody Bible
Institute. It was here, on Tuesday, October 17, 1943, a bright
autumn afternoon that he presided over the regular Board
executive committee meeting.

"I would like to take a few minutes," he began, "to talk
about the future of the Institute." President Will Houghton sat
back in his chair and listened. Henry, with the full attention of
those present, continued. "We must not overlook the drift to
modernism that is so visible in organized Christianity. As never
before, Moody Bible Institute has a responsibility to give forth
the true gospel."

One of the board members took some notes as the
silver-haired businessman continued. "There are two particular
phases of that responsibility," he told them. "First, we must
preserve sound doctrine in the years ahead." Heads nodded in
agreement. "Then," Mr. Crowell added, "we must get the gospel
to the ends of the earth. We have a large student enrollment

this year . . . there's been a significant growth in the circulation of *Moody Monthly*, and the WMBI audience is getting bigger every day. But Moody Bible Institute must think in terms of still greater things for the glory of Christ!"

Dr. Houghton sat spellbound listening to a man, nearly 90, talking about the future. The Christian statesman continued sharing his vision with the Board members for another 45 minutes, then excused himself for other duties.

At his Quaker Oats office, he made travel arrangements for a trip to Cleveland the next week.

On Sunday, October 22, he attended worship services at the Winnetka Bible Church where a friend, Rev. Milford Sholund, was a visiting minister giving the sermon. Another old friend, Gipsy Smith, with his wife, were house guests and accompanied Mr. Crowell to the service.

After church, at dinner, Smith and Mr. Crowell were comparing notes on the service. Everything was as it should be--a wonderful service, outstanding choir music, excellent sermon. "Most beautiful!" exclaimed Gipsy Smith, "and that sermon on the Second Coming, wonderful. Imagine," he said, "without dying, to be caught up in the air to meet the Lord! How wonderful."

Mr. Crowell sat quietly in thought before replying. "Yes," he answered, "that would be wonderful. But it is more wonderful, so far as I am concerned, to be raised from the dead upon Christ's appearance. For the dead in Christ shall rise *first* at His coming!"

The next day, Mr. Crowell took the commuter train to Chicago and walked the seven blocks to his office. No one seemed to notice that, for once, he seemed a bit out of breath and somewhat pale.

After awhile though, he seemed renewed by working. Then, in the afternoon, he picked up his topcoat and briefcase and headed for the elevator. He greeted the elevator operator by name and asked about his family. Mr. Crowell smiled as the man told about his weekend and important events in his life.

When the elevator stopped at the lobby, he looked at his watch and saw he was running a few minutes behind schedule. Picking up his pace, he strode toward the train station in long, quick steps. Weary and out of breath, he entered the train compartment and took a seat. He placed his briefcase on his lap and took out his *New Testament* to read.

But before he could see the words on the page, his great heart stopped. He died as the train left the station, and was ushered into eternity at once, to the complete oblivion of the other commuters.

On Thursday, October 26, 1943, much of Chicago came out to say good-bye to Henry Parsons Crowell. His funeral was held at Moody Bible Institute, in the lower level of the new Torrey-Gray Auditorium under construction.

Ironically, it was James M. Gray (one of the two men the auditorium building was named for) who said, "It was the brain and heart of H. P. Crowell that made Moody Bible Institute!"

Yet, Mr. Crowell had not permitted his name to be placed on one of the buildings, yielding to his promise to not rob God of the glory for his efforts.

The body of Mr. Crowell now lay in a casket as crowds passed by in tribute.

They came from all walks of life. Bankers and tycoons, laborers and the poor. He had touched lives in every economic and social sector. Moody students, faculty, his co-workers and those who served him. Great and small, they passed his casket and wept for this man who meant so much to so many.

They looked upon his peaceful expression as he lay in the casket, but were drawn to something in his right hand. He held his small, worn leather-bound *New Testament* in his hand, resting over his heart.

For the service, the Moody Chorale sang two favorite hymns, *For God So Loved the World* and *Still, Still With Thee.* Dr.

The Cereal Tycoon

William Culbertson, Dean of MBI, led in prayer before Dr. Will Houghton, President, gave the memorial address. As he got up to speak, his voice betrayed the emotion he felt for the man he eulogized. Here are excerpts from his address:

> *It has been my sad duty to preside at the funeral service of three great men whose lives were intertwined with that of the Moody Bible Institute--Dr. Torrey, Dr. Gray, and now Henry P. Crowell. . . . It has never been my custom to eulogize in such a service as this, for I have understood it to be the minister's responsibility to address the living and remind them that they too must go the way of all the earth. But this occasion is so unusual it will not be thought poor taste to make personal reference to this great soul, now departed.*
>
> *There is a sense in which we could be considered selfish for confining our remarks to the relationship Mr. Crowell bore to the Institute. There are other realms in which he held high place: the Quaker Oats Company, which had so many years of his life and so much of his affectionate interest, and of course the realm of his family, where he loved his children and grandchildren and was loved in return. But these friends will be understandingly sympathetic if this proves to be almost entirely a tribute to his relationship to the Moody Bible Institute.*
>
> *Henry P. Crowell was the most Christlike man I have ever met, bearing to the full that distinctive mark of the Christian--humility. He exemplified and illustrated it in his daily life and his contact with men, the life about which so many of us talk, and some of us desire. He loved men, whether or not he agreed with them. He was keen of intellect, clear in memory, and wise in judgment, even this far, in his 89th year.*
>
> *Many, many messages have been received from those who have been touched by this noble life, and who would be here today, were it possible. . . . It cannot be said that a nation mourns the passing of Mr. Crowell. He so sought to keep himself out of sight in all his work for*

Christ that comparatively few have recognized a king in disguise. Those of us who knew him saw the royalty shine through. And he would not have wanted the plaudits of the world. He would much rather have the approval of the Lord.

Without wishing to take anything from the records of past Institute leaders, in all honesty the admission must be made that this man has been more responsible than any other for the success of the Moody Bible Institute from early times to this good hour. The continuance of the school, the sending forth of multitudes of young people with the gospel to the ends of the earth, the radio ministry, and all the other varied activities, were made possible largely by the devotion and generosity of this consecrated servant of Christ.

Who can doubt that last Monday evening, among those who welcomed him in the glory were some who were there because of his part in the training of the Christian workers who brought them the gospel. Perhaps he has even had an opportunity to report to D. L. Moody on the state of the Institute. Surely he has been able to give a good account of his stewardship. . . .

But what makes possible such a character as Mr. Crowell? We understand that there are many high qualities of human goodness in the man, but we recognize also something beyond these qualities. Are there not business men--young business men--and some of our students in training, who are asking this question at the moment? The answer is clear and unmistakable. If you could ask him, his answer humbly would be in one word-- Christ.

I hold in my hands certain things taken from his pockets the day he departed. There is a poem on "Christian Victory"; a clipping, "How to Become a Christian"; a tract, "To Walk With God"; some Scripture notes in his own hand; Scripture references, and that familiar poem of Annie Johnson Flint--

The Cereal Tycoon

Christ has no hands but our hands
　　To do His work today;
He has no feet but our feet
　　To lead me in His way.
He has no tongue but our tongue
　　To tell men how He died,
He has no help but our help
　　To bring them to His side.

We are the only Bible
　　The careless world will read;
We are the sinners' gospel,
　　We are the scoffers' creed;
We are the Lord's last message,
　　Given in deed and word;
What if the type be crooked,
　　What if the print be blurred?

What if our hands are busy
　　With work that is not His;
What if our feet are walking
　　Where sin's allurement is;
What if our tongues are saying
　　Things His lips would spurn;
How can we hope to help Him,
　　Or hasten His return?

Believing in Christ as Savior at an early age, and then yielding his life to Christ, he found sustenance and joy in fellowship with Christ through His word and prayer. The great questions that determined everything in his life were, "Is this what He wants me to do?" or "Will it glorify Him?" . . .

It is selfish of us to mourn in such an hour. Of course we are going to miss him dreadfully, but there is for us the knowledge that he is with Christ. The body, to be taken to Cleveland, there to rest in Lake View Cemetery, is only the garment of the spirit, the tenement of clay in which he lived for nearly 90 years, but Henry P. Crowell still lives!

159

* * * *

One man can--and *did*--make a difference. Henry Parsons Crowell was a remarkable man.

D. L. Moody's words still echo at the turn of this new century. Moody had said, "The reason I like to think big things for God is that He deserves it. Now, whether it's evangelism, or your work, or your money. Whatever it is, you ought to think of big ways you can be used for God."

"That feller I met in Ireland, Henry Varley, told me, *'The world has yet to see what God can do with and for and through and in a man who is fully and wholly consecrated to Him'*."

The words of Moody had seemed directed to Henry Parsons Crowell. "Varley didn't say he had to be brilliant, or rich, or anything else. A *man*. Just *a man!* Well, I told God, that with the Holy Spirit in me, *I'll* be that man. And what about you? Will you be one of those men? Is your God worthy of such a commitment?"

Henry Crowell became that kind of man and the world *did* get to see what God can do through such a man.

Will our contemporary world get the chance to see the difference that *one person wholly committed to God* can make in his or her world *in the 21st Century?*